Tapping the Power of Nonfiction

Lucy Calkins, Series Editor

Katie Clements

Photography by Peter Cunningham

HEINEMANN ◆ PORTSMOUTH, NH

To Alyna, Marie, and Yana—our conversations about teaching have sustained and inspired me from the very beginning.

Heinemann
361 Hanover Street
Portsmouth, NH 03801–3912
www.heinemann.com

Offices and agents throughout the world

The author and publisher wish to thank those who have generously given permission to reprint borrowed material:

Approximately 2,340 words from *Fast Food Nation: The Dark Side of the All American Meal*, by Eric Schlosser, Mariner Books and Penguin Books Ltd. Copyright © 2001 by Eric Schlosser. Reprinted by permission of Houghton Mifflin Harcourt Publishing Company and Penguin Random House UK.

Excerpts from "The Battle Over GMOs" by Alexandra Potenza, from *The New York Times Upfront*, February 8, 2016. Copyright © 2016 by Scholastic Inc. Reprinted by permission of Scholastic, Inc.

Excerpts from "Genetic Engineering: A Guide for Kids" *Tiki the Penguin*. Reprinted by permission of OneWorld.

"Scientists make a better potato," by Keith Ridler, Associated Press, January 21, 2016. Copyright 2017. Associated Press. 130216:0917PF "GMO Information" from Kids Right to Know—One Planet for All, All for One Planet http://www.kidsrighttoknow.com/gmos.

Cataloging-in-Publication data is on file with the Library of Congress.

ISBN-13: 978-0-325-09724-4

Editor: Tracy Wells
Production: Elizabeth Valway
Cover and interior designs: Jenny Jensen Greenleaf
Photography: Peter Cunningham
Composition: Publishers' Design and Production Services, Inc.
Manufacturing: Steve Bernier

Printed in the United States of America on acid-free paper
21 20 19 18 17 VP 2 3 4 5

Contents

BEND III Researching a New Topic with More Independence While Helping Students to Read Critically

Registration instructions to access the digital resources that accompany this book may be found on p. x.

Acknowledgments

THIS BOOK stands on the shoulders of the Teacher College Reading and Writing Project's decades of work teaching kids how to read and love nonfiction. I'm so grateful to all my colleagues at the Project, too many to properly thank here.

None of this would have been possible without Lucy Calkins, who spearheads all the work at the Project. Lucy has an unparalleled ability to think through the big picture implications of any decision, while still considering the impact of an individual word. Lucy's feedback lifted the level of each and every session in this book, and the lessons she imparted will left the level of my writing for decades to come. She especially suggested ways to make the trickiest content accessible to all kids. I am a better reader, writer, and teacher because I get to work closely with Lucy.

The middle school staff development team at the Project played an essential role in bringing this project to life: Audra Robb, Mary Ehrenworth, Emily Strang-Campbell, Cornelius Minor, Katy Wischow, Pablo Wolfe, Heather Michael, Heather Burns, Leah Bragin Page, Michelle McGrath, Elisa Zonana, Laurie Burke, Tim Steffen, Jordan Kravitz, Dwight McCaulsky, and Kat Schechter. Many joined me in a nonfiction think tank, where they analyzed lessons, shared critical feedback, and suggested ways to streamline lessons. Special thanks to Dwight, Kat, and Laurie, who went above and beyond to coordinate and support pilot teachers.

Audra Robb, who heads all the middle school work at the Project, deserves particular thanks for helping shape this unit into something both challenging and developmentally appropriate. She and Katy Wischow provided essential feedback on the nonfiction chapter books that fill the recommended text lists. Special thanks are also due to Kelly Boland Hohne. Her innovative work planning and delivering nonfiction read-alouds helped breathe particular life into the read-aloud sections in this book. Mary Ehrenworth, Deputy Director of the Teachers College Reading and Writing Project, functioned as a critical thought partner. Even when she was deep in the throes of her own writing, she never hesitated to take time to talk with me. This book is infinitely better because of our conversations.

Many of my colleagues generously shared their time as the unit neared publication. Thank you to Jen DeSutter, Kim Fox, Eric Hand, Hannah Kolbo, and Casey Maxwell who illustrated the charts that fill these pages and will soon live in classrooms around the world. Julia Mooney deserves thanks for clarifying the trajectory of writing about reading across the unit. Curating nonfiction text sets required particular care and precision, and Katherine Miller spent countless hours reading to find the best texts for your middle schoolers. Thank you to Kelly Boland Hohne, who shared her expertise about curating text sets and was always willing to think through things with me. I'm also grateful to my colleagues who read through draft text sets and shared feedback. I am lucky to have such generous and insightful friends.

Heinemann's entire team worked to bring these pages to life. Anna Gratz Cockerille, editor extraordinaire, went above and beyond in her role. She fine-tuned each sentence, drafted needed content, and near the end, suggested a way to reorder sessions that brought a special cohesion to the unit. Tracy Wells, Supervising Editor, joined the book early on and again at the home stretch, and her careful attention to detail helped pull everything in the book together.

Abby Heim heads all of the Project's work with Heinemann. She helped to keep this project on deadline and suggested ways to make the units more useful to teachers. I'm grateful to the entire staff at Heinemann, especially Elizabeth Valway, who leads the team that brought this book through the production process and organized all the online resources.

Pilot teachers and coaches played a critical role in ensuring the unit really worked: Garrett Kyle from MS 223 in Bronx, New York; Michaela Harris, Robert Foster, Rebecca Fano, and Christy O'Connor from Ridgedale Middle

School in Florham Park, New Jersey; Veronica Garcia, Clemencia Acevedo, Megan Steenrod, and Mandy Ehrlich from Urban Science Academy in Bronx, New York; and Angela Lamorgese-McDonald and Sue Mimnaugh at Hauppauge Middle School in Hauppauge, New York. Special thanks to Marc Todd from IS 289, who opened his doors to me so I could spend time learning alongside his middle schoolers. It's their students' work that brings life to these pages.

An Orientation to the Unit

NONFICTION READING SKILLS are essential to students' achievement in virtually every academic discipline. To do science, students need to read science texts, including books and articles. To study history, they need to be skilled at reading all kinds of secondary and primary sources. There is a reason that global standards have focused increasingly on nonfiction skills. When you help a child become powerful at nonfiction reading, you help that child become more powerful with school. You also foster informed citizenship, a passion for knowledge, and the lifelong joy of reading to learn.

It turns out that along with specific nonfiction reading strategies, it also makes a tremendous difference to students' success if they learn to quickly immerse themselves in a subject. This means reading whole books, or reading articles *and* visiting websites and academic videos, and opening oneself up to the complexities and nuances of a subject. The world is full of fascinating instructional texts. Kids who do well in any discipline seek these out, and they read on their own. We can help make those habits, as well as essential skills, part of every student's toolkit.

Across this unit, you'll help your students develop a solid set of nonfiction reading skills: discerning central ideas, summarizing to create a concise version of a text, synthesizing within and across texts, building vocabulary, growing ideas, and reading critically to question the author's point of view and perspective. At the same time, you'll teach students to develop flexibility as they read across text types, reading a variety of nonfiction chapter books, articles, trade books, and online resources, and as they transfer what they know from one text type to the next. Students will learn to build up their background knowledge, so they aren't intimidated by unfamiliar texts and topics, but instead have skills to confidently read and learn from those texts. Along the way, you'll teach in ways that build students' love for nonfiction reading, by modeling your own fascination with topics, supporting students with growing their own ideas, and giving them time to work collaboratively around texts and topics of interest. Expect for your students to leave this unit as more confident readers of nonfiction, able to read slightly harder texts, and eager to weave nonfiction reading into their independent reading lives.

This unit is designed to be a second unit in a year's work in the Units of Study for Teaching Reading in Middle School series. The sessions that follow assume you have a reading workshop up and running in your classroom and that your students have already done some work in reading partnerships. If you taught *A Deep Study of Character* first, your students will be fully equipped to dive into this unit. If you chose to begin the year some other way, you might set aside a few class periods to launch your reading workshop, diving into the lessons that begin *A Deep Study of Character* for ideas as to how to get your reading workshop running strong. If you are a content teacher, there is a small section for you on page ix, on adapting these teaching points to your content studies.

OVERVIEW OF THE UNIT

This book consists of three major bends, or parts, each with their own distinct focus. Each bend is designed to last five to eight days, although you may choose to extend a bend by a day or so if there is a critical skill you want to give your students more practice with.

In Bend I: Navigating Nonfiction Chapter Books in Book Clubs, with an Emphasis on Discerning Central Ideas, you'll invite students to read nonfiction chapter books in book clubs. Reading longer nonfiction texts presents a host of challenges that may be new to your students, so your first read-aloud will tackle this head on, emphasizing the work readers do when they read the front matter in nonfiction chapter books. You'll teach students to get an initial sense of their texts' central ideas and then to hold their initial ideas loosely, remaining open to the fact that those central ideas may need to be revised in light of new information as they read on. You'll help students consider the ways in which embedded stories fit with the central ideas in a text. Of course, it also matters that students develop their own ideas, so you'll teach them that nonfiction readers read to be fascinated, and that they generate questions and ideas that spark rich conversation and bring those to their clubs, resulting in deeper conversations. As Bend I culminates, you'll invite students to self-assess their practice using anchor charts and to set goals for what they'll work on moving forward.

Then, in Bend II: Investigating Topics with Research Groups, and Synthesizing across Texts on That Topic, students will work in research groups to study nonfiction topics they select from a small set of options you provide. You'll teach students that when researchers begin studying a new topic, it helps to preview texts to notice repeating subtopics and then to read easier texts first, since those texts often give readers access to critical vocabulary and concepts. Then, you'll teach students how to synthesize across texts, so they consider how the new information they are learning fits with, extends, or contradicts what they already know. As part of this, you'll support students with building their vocabularies and summarizing texts to hold on to their central ideas. This bend is also about empowering students to solve their own problems, so you'll teach students that when they encounter something unfamiliar in their texts, they can do a bit of on-the-run research to build up their knowledge, rather than raising their hands or appealing to you, the teacher, for help. At the end of Bend II, I suggest you put aside a bit of time to celebrate all your students have learned by inviting them to curate their own text sets on their topic. These text sets can then become the starter text sets used by the new research groups in Bend III.

Finally, in Bend III: Researching a New Topic with More Independence While Helping Students to Read Critically, you'll invite students to research a new topic in their research groups. Rather than reteaching students how to launch their research, you'll remind students of their earlier learning and send them off to transfer all they've learned about researching well to their new topics. To extend this work, you'll introduce students to the special challenges readers face while researching online, and you'll suggest strategies readers can use to overcome these challenges as they study online articles, interactive text features, and videos. You'll also support students in reading critically, by equipping them with strategies to discern an author's point of view and to determine whether a text is trustworthy. To celebrate all your students have learned, you'll invite them to create and deliver their own TED-style talks that capture a few key points related to their topic. And, you'll help them consider ways they can sustain their nonfiction reading lives moving forward, even as you transition into a new reading unit.

ASSESSMENT

You'll want to plan for how you'll assess students within this unit. If you have students reading significantly below grade level, you might decide to do running records in nonfiction to ensure those students are appropriately matched with nonfiction texts. Often, though not always, students are a level or two lower as nonfiction readers than they are as fiction readers. Fountas and Pinnell have a set of nonfiction running records that are particularly useful for determining students' nonfiction reading levels.

You might decide to give a brief performance assessment to your students, perhaps highlighting one skill that you know is critically important within the unit. You could develop a question tied to that skill, choose a short nonfiction text where students can practice the skill, and then set aside 15 or 20 minutes for an assessment. For instance, you could ask, "What are the central ideas of this text? How does the author convey the central ideas?" and then give students an excerpt from *Fast Food Nation: The Dark Side of the All-American Meal* to read and determine the central ideas of. If you are teaching this unit in the content areas, you might decide to use a text that matches content your students know well. Of course, you could decide to expand the assessment and develop questions around other key skills that are taught in the unit, such as synthesizing across texts, determining an author's perspective, and growing ideas.

Across the unit, you'll want to assess your students regularly and use your observations to guide your conferences, small-group work, and whole-class instruction. You might study students' reader's notebooks with the lens of major skills of the unit, noticing whether students are revising their thinking about central ideas as they read of synthesizing across texts on a topic. Similarly, you could study students' book club and research group talk, noting both the talk moves kids make and the reading skill work kids engage with as they talk. Make these assessments informal, brief, and ongoing, and follow up your observations with some targeted teaching that moves kids forward as readers. The conferring and small-group work sections across the unit will be helpful as you plan for this instruction.

GETTING READY

The success of this unit hinges on having enough texts to keep your students engaged and reading just-right texts across all twenty sessions. All too often, students' volume of reading drops dramatically during nonfiction reading units, and students crawl through just a few pages of text a day. To counter this, you'll want to spend some time before this unit begins gathering texts.

For Bend I of this unit, students read nonfiction chapter books in book clubs. You'll want to group students roughly by reading level, and then match each club with high-interest, accessible books they can read. I recommend you use students' fiction reading levels as a starting point when matching them with nonfiction texts. Clubs reading at level U and above will probably read one book across the bend. Clubs reading at level T and below might read two or more books. For instance, a club of four students reading *The Omnivore's Dilemma: The Secret Behind What You Eat, Young Readers Edition* by Michael Pollan, which is a level X, will need four copies of the book, one for each student. Students reading near a level P might read two or three books from the What Was . . . ? series, such as *What Was Hurricane Katrina?* by Robin Koontz and *What Were the Twin Towers?* by Jim O'Connor. The Nonfiction Book Clubs Shelf, available through the Teachers College Reading and Writing Project Classroom Libraries (Heinemann 2016), will be a valuable resource as you source books. Students will also need access to Post-it® notes and a reading notebook. Across Bend I, we suggest you read aloud excerpts from *Fast Food Nation: The Dark Side of the All-American Meal* by Eric Schlosser, so you'll want to secure a copy of the book if you decide to use this book as your read-aloud text. You'll find an alternate read-aloud calendar in the online resources if you decide to substitute in the young readers' edition of the book *Chew On This: Everything You Don't Want to Know About Fast Food* by Charles Wilson and Eric Schlosser.

In Bends II and III, students research fascinating topics through nonfiction text sets in research groups, comprised of around four students. They'll research social media, teen activism, atomic bombs, the *Titanic*, and more. You'll want to assemble significant starter sets of texts for each research group. Ideally, these text sets include articles, online resources, and trade books. I encourage you to order a few trade books for each research group, as having access to book-length nonfiction will go a long way in keeping all of your students reading. You'll find suggested texts available on the online resources that you can download and print for students or make available to students electronically. At the same time, you'll research a topic alongside your students, reading across a collection of articles, trade books, and online sources. I recommend you research genetically modified organisms, as this topic is embedded into each minilesson across Bends II and III. In the online resources, you'll find a set of recommended texts on this topic that you can print and use. You can also find more information about provisioning your students with the necessary resources in the letters that begin Bends I, II, and III.

To help students keep track of their reading volume, you might ask them to continue the reading logs they began in *A Deep Study of Character* during Bend I of this unit. When students transition to reading shorter texts, you might ask them to instead keep a running list of articles read or a tally of pages read per day.

A NOTE FOR CONTENT TEACHERS ON ADAPTING THIS INSTRUCTION WITHIN CONTENT UNITS

Some of you who are holding this book right now are social studies or science teachers, and you're wondering how you might fold some of this instruction into your content studies. First, know that it will be a gift to your students if they not only fall in love with your content, but also learn how to study that content. Social studies students who know more about how to go about reading to learn will do better in social studies. Science students who learn how to learn science from a rich variety of sources are more likely to be able to continue their studies.

Here are a few tips for weaving some of this instruction into your content units. First, you'll want to choose one part, or bend of the unit, for any given content unit, rather than attempt to move through this entire reading unit in the course of one content unit. Second, you'll want to consider the kind of reading your students will do in each of your content units. So, for instance, if you plan to teach a content unit on the American Revolution, during which students will read biographies, that could be a great unit to tuck in a lot of the teaching from Bend I of this reading unit, which invites students to read longer nonfiction books. On the other hand, if you are in a science unit on climate change in which students will mostly read articles and websites, the teaching of Bend II will be a better match. A third tip is to find out if your ELA teachers are also teaching nonfiction, in which case you can remind students of some of that learning, or if the primary nonfiction instruction in your school will happen in social studies, in which case you might want to map out three units across the year where kids can do a lot of reading in social studies. And the final tip is—put some time into building up content libraries. It's easier to teach reading research skills when there is a lot of great content to read.

ONLINE DIGITAL RESOURCES

A variety of resources to accompany this unit of study are available in the online resources, including charts and examples of student work shown throughout *Tapping the Power of Nonfiction*, as well as links to other electronic resources. Offering daily support for your teaching, these materials will help you provide a structured learning environment that fosters independence and self-direction.

To access and download all the digital resources for *Tapping the Power of Nonfiction*:

1. Go to www.heinemann.com and click the link in the upper right to log in. (If you do not have an account yet, you will need to create one.)

2. Enter the following registration code in the box to register your product: MSRUOS_DWFL2.

3. Enter the security information requested.

4. Once you have registered your product it will appear in the list of My Online Resources.

(You may keep copies of these resources on up to six of your own computers or devices. By downloading the file you acknowledge that they are for your individual or classroom use and that neither the resources nor the product code will be distributed or shared.)

READ-ALOUD PACING GUIDE

BEND I	Read-Aloud Text: *Fast Food Nation* by Eric Schlosser
Session 1 Read-Aloud	Skim the cover and the table of contents then read aloud from the Introduction.
Session 2	Read aloud a selection from Chapter 1.
Session 3	Read aloud a selection from Chapter 2.
Session 4	Read aloud a selection from Chapter 3.
Session 5	Read aloud a selection from Chapter 3.
Session 6	Read aloud a selection from Chapter 2. Share a different selection from Chapter 2 for students' practice.
Session 7	
BEND II	**Read-Aloud Texts:** A selection of articles and digital texts about GMOs
Session 8 Read-Aloud	Preview and then read aloud a selection from the article "The Battle Over GMOs" by Alexandra Potenza. Preview and then read aloud from an easy text, such as the article "So What Is Genetic Engineering?"
Session 9	Read aloud a selection from the article "The Battle Over GMOs."
Session 10	Revisit selections from "The Battle Over GMOs."
Session 11	Show the video "Seeing Red: The Flavr Savr Tomato."
Session 12	Read aloud a selection from "The Battle Over GMOs."
Session 13	
Session 14	Read aloud a selection from "The Battle Over GMOs."
Session 15	
BEND III	**Read-Aloud Texts:** A selection of articles and digital texts about GMOs
Session 16	
Session 17	Read aloud from the Just Label It! website.
Session 18 Read-Aloud	Read aloud from the article "Labels for GMO Foods Are a Bad Idea." Read aloud from the article, "Scientists Make a Better Potato."
Session 19	Read aloud from the article, "What's a GMO?" Revisit "The Battle Over GMOs." Share the article "GMO Information."
Session 20	Show students clips of TED talks, such as those by Chimamanda Ngozi Adichie, Ben Kacyra, or Christien Meindertsma.

Navigating Nonfiction Chapter Books in Book Clubs, with an Emphasis on Discerning Central Ideas

A Letter to Teachers

ear Teachers,

The first bend of this nonfiction reading unit prepares students for a couple of challenges. For starters, it matters that students learn to read longer nonfiction texts. In fiction reading units, your students probably read twenty pages in school and twenty pages at home a day, but when nonfiction reading units begin, those same students' volume typically plunges as they spend an entire class plodding their way through a two-page article. Richard Allington, in his book *Summer Reading: Closing the Rich/Poor Achievement Gap* (2012), explains that for every five weeks students don't read enough, they drop a reading level. This means that careful attention to reading volume *matters*. One way you'll tackle this head-on across this bend is by provisioning students with longer nonfiction chapter books, ensuring that they read a book, not an article, during the bend. You'll also support practices that lead to engaged reading: grouping students into book clubs, teaching students to react to their reading with fascination and wonder, and encouraging them to read other texts that complement their club book.

It also matters that you equip students with strategies for what to do when texts get longer. Nell Duke, a researcher at the University of Michigan who studies student resiliency, notes that 60% of college students are dropping out of "hard" majors in college. Duke found that a major reason why students were leaving these majors was because they struggled when required to read longer nonfiction texts. Reading longer nonfiction texts, such as long journal articles, is significantly different than reading shorter articles. Within this bend, you'll provision students with high-interest, accessible nonfiction chapter books, and you'll begin to support students' resiliency by teaching them how to use their classmates and other available resources to grow ideas.

Depending on your schedule, and how often you have reading workshop, this bend will take you about a week and a half, with each session lasting one day. Similar to other units in this series, you launch the work with a read-aloud where you get some of the major work of the bend going, teaching kids how their reading work needs to change as they begin to read nonfiction chapter books. The book we use here is *Fast Food Nation: The Dark Side of the All-American Meal* by Eric Schlosser (2001), which examines the way fast food has altered life in America, from health to food production to the poverty gap. It's a long book, so you won't be able to read aloud the whole text in class. Instead, you'll begin by reading the introduction to lay the foundation for the book and to teach students how to read this fascinating—and challenging—part of their nonfiction texts. In subsequent minilessons, you'll move through very brief and engaging excerpts that give students a sense of the book as a whole and get them fascinated by the topic.

Across this bend, your students will work in book clubs. Book clubs typically contain an even number of students, ideally two sets of partners. You'll want to group students into book clubs prior to Session 1 and provision each club with a text that students can read with accuracy, fluency, and comprehension. Clubs will probably consist of kids reading at or near the same reading level, though you'll also want to take their interests and social dynamics into account. They'll meet nearly every day, typically at the end of the session. The amount of time they'll have to talk will depend on the length of your reading periods. See more on scheduling for book clubs in *A Guide to the Reading Workshop: Middle School Grades*. Each club will read at least one longer nonfiction chapter book, and you'll want to choose high-interest books that are accessible to your students—that is, ones they can read well. You may want them to read books such as *Quiet Power: The Secret Strength of Introverted Kids*; *Bomb: The Race to Build—and Steal—the World's Most Dangerous Weapon*; *World Without Fish*; or *Julius Caesar: Dictator for Life*. We've included a list of suggested nonfiction chapter books in the online resources, at both benchmark and below-benchmark levels. Of course, a club could read *Fast Food Nation*, and they'd benefit from the extra support of hearing you work with text excerpts during minilessons.

You'll see some books we suggest are *au courant*, high-interest nonfiction books, whereas others relate to critical topics in science and social studies. Keep an eye on reading level as you match kids with books. Kids who read significantly below grade level might read several nonfiction books across this bend, whereas students reading adult-level nonfiction texts might only read one book. We recommend you do whatever you can to get your students their own copies of texts so they can annotate them and keep them afterward, replicating ways they'll mark up texts in high school and college.

If your students have grown up with the Units of Study, they probably have been in book clubs since second grade, so you'll want to reference what they already know about working in clubs and build on that. Refer to the section on book clubs in *A Guide to the Reading Workshop: Middle School Grades* for more tips on getting book clubs going quickly and effectively. Across this first bend, you'll remind students of the importance of coming to book clubs prepared with annotations and possible discussion points. You'll help students balance their reading and writing time, so they move through a volume of text while still jotting interesting thoughts, and you'll teach them to set ambitious reading goals. You'll also coach to lift the level of club conversations. As you support book clubs, keep in mind the goal for clubs is to function independently of you, so you'll want to coach with a light touch, adding tips without taking over the conversation and then removing yourself so students get to continue the conversation without you. Again, you'll find the *Guide* a helpful resource.

As always, feel free to alter the texts you use in this unit, such as the read-aloud text, although you'll find this takes some significant work, as particular excerpts of the read-aloud text are embedded in each session. If you do choose to work with different texts, look for engaging nonfiction chapter books with related digital texts (documentaries are ideal). Keep in mind that your text selections should pique students' interest in the genre, so look for well-written nonfiction texts with topics that will appeal to a wide range of students.

All the best,
Katie

Read-Aloud

Reading with Engagement and Fascination
Right from the Introduction

<table>
<tr><td colspan="2">IN THIS SESSION</td></tr>
<tr>
<td>TODAY, THROUGH READ-ALOUD, YOU'LL teach students that readers orient themselves to a nonfiction text by reading the front matter closely to formulate questions and grow initial ideas.</td>
<td>TODAY YOUR STUDENTS will spend most of the session participating in the read-aloud, and then will meet briefly in their clubs to receive their book-club books and begin reading.</td>
</tr>
</table>

CONNECTION

Invite students to sit in the meeting area with their book clubs. Generate excitement for the work of the new unit and the ways in which students will outgrow themselves as readers.

I projected a list of students grouped by book club, and I asked them to find a seat in the meeting area next to the other kids in their club. Then, I said, "Readers, today we're diving into a new unit of study focused on reading nonfiction texts, where we'll investigate and become experts on really fascinating topics. And I've been wracking my brain to figure out what you might read. I know in the past, you read a ton of short articles, and you worked to put what you read in one short article together with what you learned in other short articles, and that gave you lots of ideas about the topic you were studying.

"But, here's the thing: you're not *Time for Kids* readers anymore. By now, you're pros at reading those short, three-paragraph articles, where the author pretty much comes right out in the heading and tells you what the article will be about and where the content is all super-straightforward. That work is pretty simple for you now. Instead of going back to the same ol' texts you've been reading

GETTING READY

✔ Prepare your read-aloud (we recommend *Fast Food Nation*) by marking places in the text where you'll stop and think aloud and where you'll ask students to turn and talk. You'll find printable Post-it notes in the online resources that you can add to your book. 👆

✔ Before this session, select a longer nonfiction chapter book that's high-interest and accessible for each book club, and prepare a short sales pitch for each book to help get clubs excited about their books. See the online resources for a list of possible titles. 👆

✔ Create and display a list of students by book club, so clubs can choose a spot together in the meeting area. Students will talk with partners in their clubs, so you may want to set up these partnerships in advance (see Connection).

✔ If possible, prepare to display relevant sections of the demonstration text for clubs to work with during the read-aloud (see Conducting the Read-Aloud).

✔ Prepare to display images of Cheyenne Mountain and the Cheyenne Mountain Air Force Station (see Conducting the Read-Aloud). 👆

✔ Prepare an anchor chart titled "To Make the Most of Your Nonfiction Chapter Books . . ." (see Link). 👆

✔ Leave Post-it flags on each table (see Link).

for years, I thought you and the new book club you're sitting with might be game to take on the challenge of reading longer nonfiction chapter books, the kind of books that many avid readers of nonfiction really love, books like *The Port Chicago 50*, *Malala*, and *Courage Has No Color*.

"If you're game, we'll study how the thinking you do when you read across many, many pages is pretty significantly different from the kind of thinking you do when reading an article. Are you up for it?"

The kids signaled yes, and I nodded. "Great, because learning how to read books like these will prepare you to confidently read any longer nonfiction text you encounter in your future, whether it's a chapter book you want to read about your favorite soccer team, a journal article you're required to read for a college course, or a long passage on the ACT. And, once you can read any nonfiction text, there's no limit to what you can learn and what you can be.

"You and your club will get other nonfiction books to read, but I chose a book for us to read aloud. It's called *Fast Food Nation: The Dark Side of the All-American Meal*. I know you might be thinking, 'Seriously? A book about fast food? Couldn't you choose a more compelling topic?' But I think you'll soon see that nonfiction authors often take seemingly ordinary topics—fish, salt, latitude and longitude lines, even snowmen—and craft powerful books you won't want to put down."

CONDUCTING THE READ-ALOUD

Demonstrate how you orient yourself to the read-aloud text, then channel students to talk with a partner in their book club to consider what the text might teach.

"Ready to give this a try? Let's do what readers typically do when reading a nonfiction book, and take a minute to orient ourselves to the text, to anticipate what it might teach. I'll show you how I study the front cover first, and then you'll preview the table of contents." I displayed the front cover and thought aloud. "Hmm, . . . I see a map of the United States printed on a French fry box with the words *Fast Food Nation* on it, so the author might be talking about how the United States is a place that eats a lot of fast food. And the author must not think this is all good because it says, 'the dark side of the all-American meal' and because this *New York Times* quote on the top mentions how we can't continue 'eating fast food in blissful ignorance.'

"I'm going to display the table of contents. Will you and a partner in your book club look across the table of contents, and talk to each other about what you think the text might teach?" I gave students a minute to talk.

Pausing the kids' conversation, I said, "I agree. It looks like the book is divided into two big parts, one all about how the United States has eaten fast food for a long time and another about how fast food—the 'meat and potatoes'—isn't that healthy. And the chapter 'What's in the Meat' jumped out to you. One of you said

Particularly at the start of a unit, it's important to connect big unit goals to work students have done in the past. Both in nonfiction reading and when getting ready to learn something new, activating prior knowledge helps students start at the strongest possible place.

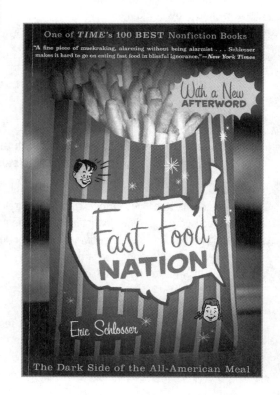

One of *TIME*'s 100 BEST Nonfiction Books

"A fine piece of muckraking, alarming without being alarmist . . . Schlosser makes it hard to go on eating fast food in blissful ignorance."—*New York Times*

With a New AFTERWORD

Fast Food NATION

Eric Schlosser

The Dark Side of the All-American Meal

you hope it's just *meat* that's in the meat, but the chapter title makes you nervous that other things may be in there too. Studying the front cover and table of contents gives us ideas about what the text might teach."

Explain that nonfiction books often get readers engaged from the beginning, but may not lay out central ideas. Ask students to formulate thoughts and questions as you read.

"In the longer chapter books you're reading now, authors rarely begin by teaching about the book's big, or central, ideas in a neat, organized way. They won't say, 'The first thing I want to teach you is . . .' and then teach all about that thing. Instead, authors often use the front matter in their books—the preludes, prefaces, prologues, forewords, and even the introductory chapters or paragraphs—to hook you on the topic, to lay out a bunch of tentative ideas, to spark questions in your mind.

"All this means that it usually takes a bit more thinking work to orient yourself to a longer nonfiction book than to a short article. To try to figure out what the text is going to be about, you might think about what's fascinating and wonder about things you don't quite understand yet. Then, you can carry those thoughts and questions with you as you read and later as you join your club conversations.

"Let's start reading the introduction. The author is going to try to get us hooked right away, so likely we'll be fascinated by the details in ways that make us want to keep reading. And, if this book is like most great nonfiction books, we'll have a whole lot of questions. As I read, let the text raise questions and spark ideas for you. I'll do the same."

I started reading aloud the introduction to *Fast Food Nation* (see page 8), displaying images of Cheyenne Mountain and of the Cheyenne Mountain Air Force Station as I read so kids could picture it.

Channel students to share their initial thinking. Then, demonstrate how you ask a question and try out a possible answer.

"Quick, share with your partner what you're thinking or wondering." I listened while students talked for about thirty seconds.

I pulled them back together and said, "This is kind of crazy, right? Hidden deep inside this mountain in Colorado, there's this huge complex that can survive an earthquake or a nuclear bomb *and* that can detect any missile, anywhere in the world, *before* it's fired? Wow! I'm wondering what kind of top-secret work takes place there that has to be so well protected, aren't you? It must be super-important if they have 1,500 people working there.

contents

Table of contents from *Fast Food Nation*

Introduction

Cheyenne Mountain sits on the eastern slope of Colorado's Front Range, rising steeply from the prairie and overlooking the city of Colorado Springs. From a distance, the mountain appears beautiful and serene, dotted with rocky outcroppings, scrub oak, and ponderosa pine. It looks like the backdrop of an old Hollywood western, yet another gorgeous Rocky Mountain vista. And yet Cheyenne Mountain is hardly pristine. One of the nation's most important military installations lies deep within it, housing units of the North American Aerospace Command, the Air Force Space Command, and the United States Space Command. During the mid-1950s, high-level officials at the Pentagon worried that America's air defenses had become vulnerable to sabotage and attack. Cheyenne Mountain was chosen as the site for a top-secret, underground combat operations center. The mountain was hollowed out, and fifteen buildings, most of them three stories high, were erected amid a maze of tunnels and passageways extending for miles. The four-and-a-half acre underground complex was designed to survive a direct hit by an atomic bomb. Now officially called the Cheyenne Mountain Air Force Station, the facility is entered through steel blast doors that are three feet thick and weigh twenty-five tons each; they automatically swing shut in less than twenty seconds. The base is closed to the public, and a heavily armed quick response team guards against intruders. Pressurized air within the complex prevents contamination by radioactive fallout and biological weapons. The buildings are mounted on gigantic steel springs to ride out an earthquake or the blast wave of a thermonuclear strike. The hallways and staircases are painted slate gray, the ceilings are low, and there are combination locks on many of the doors. A narrow escape tunnel, entered through a metal hatch, twists and turns its way out of the mountain through solid rock. The place feels like the set of an early James Bond movie, with men in jumpsuits driving little electric vans from one brightly lit cavern to another.

Fifteen hundred people work inside the mountain, maintaining the facility and collecting information from a worldwide network of radars, spy satellites, ground-based sensors, airplanes, and blimps. The Cheyenne Mountain Operations Center tracks every manmade object that enters North American airspace or that orbits the earth. It is the heart of the nation's early warning system. It can detect the firing of a long-range missile, anywhere in the world, before that missile has left the launch pad.

"I heard a lot of you saying, 'This is gonna be about fast food? Really?' One way to push your thinking is to consider possible answers to the questions the text raises for you. I had a similar question as a lot of you: How does this part fit with the topic of this book?

"Will you watch as I push myself to consider how this part could *maybe, possibly* fit? Hmm, . . . I know it *must* connect somehow, because Eric Schlosser chose to begin with this for a reason. Readers, when I'm really not sure of the answer, it helps me to say, 'Maybe . . .' or 'Perhaps . . .' That's probably the same for you too, right? Maybe it's that fast food is served there, and all the people who work there every day have to eat it? Or, perhaps some of the top-secret information they gather and protect is about the fast food industry?"

Continue reading on in the text, and channel students to listen, alert for parts that answer questions or spark new ones. Give students time to talk about their ideas, and then share a tip.

"Let's keep reading with our questions in mind, because that's what readers often do. I'm going to read on with my question in mind, how Cheyenne Mountain could possibly fit with fast food. Will you keep your questions in mind as I read? See if you get answers to those questions or if the details in the text spark new questions for you." I continued reading the introduction aloud.

Many students (and adults, for that matter!) have a harder time sustaining attention when reading nonfiction than when reading fiction. Particularly if you have English language learners or struggling readers in your class, you made need to pause your reading more often to ensure students are holding on to the information. You might do this by quickly summarizing when you pause, or by giving students more opportunities to turn and talk about what they are learning.

This futuristic military base inside a mountain has the capability to be self-sustaining for at least one month. Its generators can produce enough electricity to power a city the size of Tampa, Florida. Its underground reservoirs hold millions of gallons of water; workers sometimes traverse them in rowboats. The complex has its own underground fitness center, a medical clinic, a dentist's office, a barbershop, a chapel, and a cafeteria. When the men and women stationed at Cheyenne Mountain get tired of the food in the cafeteria, they often send somebody over to the Burger King at Fort Carson, a nearby army base. Or they call Domino's.

Almost every night, a Domino's deliveryman winds his way up the lonely Cheyenne Mountain Road, past the ominous DEADLY FORCE AUTHORIZED signs, past the security checkpoint at the entrance of the base, driving toward the heavily guarded North Portal, tucked behind chain link and barbed wire. Near the spot where the road heads straight into the mountainside, the delivery man drops off his pizzas and collects his tip. And should Armageddon come, should a foreign enemy someday shower the United States with nuclear warheads, laying waste to the whole continent, entombed within Cheyenne Mountain, along with the high-tech marvels, the pale blue jumpsuits, comic books, and Bibles, future archeologists may find other clues to the nature of our civilization—Big King wrappers, hardened crusts of Cheesy Bread, Barbeque Wing bones, and the red, white, and blue of a Domino's pizza box.

"Okay readers, I might have a better sense of how this part fits with the topic. Maybe it's that even though Cheyenne Mountain is a top-secret place, where you probably need super-high security clearance to be able to enter, the workers there like fast food so much that fast food delivery people just come and go all the time. Perhaps Eric Schlosser is showing how important fast food is to all parts of our society.

"What about you? Have any of your questions been answered? Did this part raise any new questions for you?" I gave students a few seconds to think, and then continued. "Tell your partner what you're thinking."

As students turned and talked, I coached, saying things like:

- "Tell your partner what questions you were holding in your mind as we read."

- "See if you can try on possible answers together. Try saying, 'Maybe . . .' or 'Perhaps . . .'"

- "Did the text raise new questions for you? Explain what you're thinking to each other."

Read on, thinking aloud about how specific details in the text spark ideas for you.

"I'm dying to read on, aren't you? Remember, in addition to having a lot of questions, another way to orient yourself to the text is to let the text spark ideas for you. Keep your questions in mind as I read to see if they get answered, and keep listening also for fascinating parts, the parts that spark ideas."

I continued reading.

On read-aloud days, we channel students to try multiple strategies at once, emulating the work that readers actually do when they read.

What We Eat

OVER THE LAST THREE DECADES, fast food has infiltrated every nook and cranny of American society. An industry that began with a handful of modest hot dog and hamburger stands in southern California has spread to every corner of the nation, selling a broad range of foods wherever paying customers may be found. Fast food is now served at restaurants and drive-throughs, at stadiums, airports, zoos, high schools, elementary schools, and universities, on cruise ships, trains, and airplanes, at K-Marts, Wal-Marts, gas stations, and even at hospital cafeterias. In 1970, Americans spent about $6 billion on fast food; in 2000, they spent more than $110 billion. Americans now spend more money on fast food than on higher education, personal computers, computer software, or new cars. They spend more on fast food than on movies, books, magazines, newspapers, videos, and recorded music—combined.

Pull open the glass door, feel the rush of cool air, walk in, get on line, study the backlit color photographs above the counter, place your order, hand over a few dollars, watch teenagers in uniforms pushing various buttons, and moments later take hold of a plastic tray full of food wrapped in colored paper and cardboard. The whole experience of buying fast food has become so routine, so thoroughly unexceptional and mundane, that it is now taken for granted, like brushing your teeth or stopping for a red light. It has become a social custom as American as a small, rectangular, hand-held, frozen, and reheated apple pie.

This book is about fast food, the values it embodies, and the world it has made. Fast food has proven to be a revolutionary force in American life; I am interested in it both as a commodity and as a metaphor. What people eat (or don't eat) has always been determined by a complex interplay of social, economic, and technological forces. The early Roman Republic was fed by its citizen-farmers; the Roman Empire, by its slaves. A nation's diet can be more revealing than its art or literature. On any given day in the United States about one-quarter of the adult population visits a fast food restaurant. During a relatively brief period of time, the fast food industry has helped to transform not only the American diet, but also our landscape, economy, workforce, and popular culture. Fast food and its consequences have become inescapable, regardless of whether you eat it twice a day, try to avoid it, or have never taken a single bite.

"I bet a lot of parts jumped out at you while we were reading. They did for me. Will you watch the way I take one of those parts and grow my thinking about it?

"I'm particularly fascinated by this part: that Americans spend more money on fast food than on higher education—on college and graduate schools. People always talk about college as so expensive, so it's a real shock to me that people spend more on fast food than on college. Now let me push myself to some possible ideas about it. This is making me think that fast food is perhaps a bigger part of our culture than maybe I first realized. I'm also realizing that fast food seems inexpensive when you just have it once, but people don't realize how quickly the costs add up. So maybe there's this lack of understanding when it comes to fast food in our society.

"Will you give this a try right now with your partner? Name a part that fascinates you, and tell each other some of the ideas you're having. You might use phrases like I did to grow your thinking, like 'This is making me think . . .' and 'I'm realizing . . .'"

I gave students a few minutes to talk while I coached in, encouraging them to grow their thinking:

- "That's such an interesting part, I agree. Spend a few more moments talking about it before you move on to another part, and see if you can come up with some new ideas."

- "Try saying, 'I'm realizing . . .' or 'This makes me think . . .' to grow your thinking about that idea."

- "Interesting, it seems you have not only ideas but also questions about that part. Another great way to grow ideas is to continue to ask questions. Asking questions and growing ideas often go hand in hand."

LINK

Begin an anchor chart that captures the work modeled in the read-aloud.

"I know you're all dying to keep reading *Fast Food Nation*, and we'll get to read more over the next week and a half. That's what happens when you take time to orient yourself to the text by reading all that fascinating front matter in ways that spark questions and ideas. You notice lots of surprising details that push you to think and get you hooked. I jotted some of the big work we did on a new chart."

After this session, you may be thinking, "Wow, we have a lot of work to do." Nonetheless, keep your tone celebratory and encouraging to rally your students to take on the challenges posed by this new unit.

ANCHOR CHART

To Make the Most of Your
Nonfiction Chapter Books . . .

- Orient yourself to the text.
  - Review the front cover and table of contents.
  - Read the front matter to spark questions and ideas.

To Make the Most of Your Nonfiction Chapter Books

Orient yourself.
Generate questions
and ideas.

Send students off to begin reading their nonfiction books with their clubs, paying particular attention to front matter.

"You and your club will only have about ten minutes of time to read. You'll need to find a spot around the room where your book club will meet and read. I'm going to bring around copies of a book that I chose especially for your club. While you're waiting, you could talk about some of the books you've read recently and loved.

"When you get your book, jump right into all the good stuff at the start of the book: the front and back covers, the table of contents, the front matter, or the introductory chapter if your book doesn't have other front matter. Remember that authors are using these parts to get you hooked, so notice the surprising details that spark questions in your minds.

"I left some Post-its on your desks, so if you come across a fascinating detail, flag it so you can share it with your club later. Off you go with your club to find a reading spot, and then get started orienting yourself to the text!"

If this is your second unit of the year, expect that students will have internalized your routines for moving quickly from the meeting area to their reading spots. If this is not the case, help them to get transitioned and settled quickly, as they won't have much time for independent reading on this read-aloud day.

INDEPENDENT READING

Quickly Launching the Work of the Unit

You'll probably only have ten minutes or so for your students to form into clubs and read today, as your read-aloud will take about twenty-five minutes. Since today is the first day of the unit, use the independent reading time to support clubs in choosing spots to meet and getting quickly settled into reading. Move quickly from club to club, distributing the books you selected. Some clubs will naturally take to their texts and topics, while other topics might require some salesmanship. You might prepare some quick book introductions, focused on what's fascinating about the text and topic.

For instance, if you approached a group with copies of *World Without Fish* by Mark Kurlansky, you might say, "I chose this book, *World Without Fish*, especially for your group because you're all such forward thinkers, constantly thinking about how what you do will impact the future. That's what Mark Kurlansky does in this book. And I think you'll find that fish, like fast food, are more fascinating and important than you might originally think. Something I bet you'll love about this book is how the author presents information. Flip through your copy for a minute. Doesn't he have a cool style? See how the book is filled with images? Oh, and do you notice the comics? He put comics at the end of each chapter."

If you see students diving into their books without previewing, reference the anchor chart and remind them to pause for a minute to orient themselves before reading. If clubs are just talking instead of reading, coach them to pick up their books and begin orienting themselves to the text.

SHARE

Sharing Fascinating Details and Thoughts about Your Reading

"You're all deep into getting oriented to your book, maybe even reading that first chapter, so we just have a moment for a share. Will you tell your fellow club members about any interesting details you came across?

What kind of thinking have you been doing about those details? Be sure to put a couple of blank Post-its in your book, stuck inside the cover, so that as you read tonight, you'll be ready to jot the fascinating things you notice."

READING TO BE FASCINATED

Readers, you should read for thirty to forty minutes tonight, aiming to read twenty to thirty pages in your book. Remember that early in nonfiction chapter books, authors work to get you interested. They may outline tentative ideas, but they usually won't come right out and tell you what the book is about. This means you'll probably need to notice the surprising and unusual details the author includes, the stories the author chooses to tell, and then develop some questions and thoughts about those. Let yourself be fascinated. Be sure to flag, annotate, or jot about a few parts that were particularly fascinating so you can bring those parts to your club conversation tomorrow.

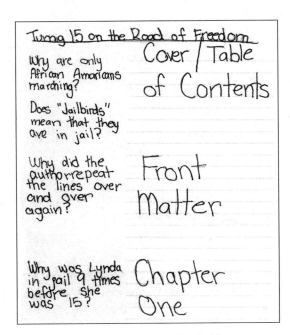

FIG. 1–1   Riya poses questions about a few
fascinating parts of her book.

Generating Questions and Ideas that Spark Rich Club Conversations

✔ Prepare to record students' thoughts about what book clubs do, using chart paper or a projected page (see Connection). 👆

✔ Choose a section of your demonstration text to show students how you mull over fascinating parts of the text to prepare for a book-club discussion. We chose pages 19–20 from *Fast Food Nation* (see Teaching and Active Engagement).

✔ While reading aloud, you might briefly show photos, possibly using a document camera, that illustrate unfamiliar concepts being discussed, such as a *carhop* (see Teaching). 👆

✔ Prepare to add to the "To Make the Most of Your Nonfiction Chapter Books . . ." anchor chart (see Link). 👆

IN THIS SESSION

TODAY YOU'LL teach students that book clubs have stronger conversations if book-club members prepare to bring significant parts that they've thought a lot about to their club conversations.

TODAY YOUR STUDENTS will practice growing their thinking about parts as they read their own books, and then will meet with their book clubs at the end of the session. In their book-club meetings, students will share significant parts they've already done some thinking about, and then they'll talk long off those parts.

MINILESSON

CONNECTION

Remind students of their previous experiences with book clubs. Ask them to generate a list of what they already know about how book clubs tend to go.

"Today will be your first book-club meeting of the year where you'll get to really talk about your books, but it likely won't be your first book-club meeting *ever*. I know you all have a bunch of experience being in book clubs. In fact, some of you have been in book clubs since you were in second grade. Will you brainstorm with your club all the things you already know about what book clubs do?" I gave students a minute to talk while I jotted what I heard them saying.

I called them back and used this as a moment to remind them of a few things they may or may not have said, but that I knew were important. I said, "I'm pretty sure most of you already know that a book club meets regularly at the end of the reading workshop." I briefly talked through the "Book clubs . . ."chart.

Share a story from your own book club as an example, then segue into the teaching point.

"Sometimes, I meet in a book club with other teachers from this school. The other day, we talked about what *we* do when we talk about texts together, and we realized that sometimes our conversations aren't great. Sometimes it seems like we keep going round and round, with each of us basically saying the same thing. For those of you who have been in book clubs before, has that ever happened to you?"

I paused for a moment, while some students nodded.

"We decided to study our talk. What we noticed was that our talk was pretty low level. We just retold what happened, or repeated the interesting facts—and that might be a fine way to get started, but we didn't really go anywhere from there. We never did the thinking about parts that you guys were doing yesterday, when we thought about stuff like how people spend more on fast food than college. We just *said* the facts, over and over and over. We didn't come prepared with anything more interesting to talk about.

"So the teachers and I made a vow that we'd get better at talking about our books. Can I teach you about what we did to get better, and you can let me know if any of that might help you?" The students nodded.

❖ Name the teaching point.

"Today I want to teach you that the quality of your book-club conversations has everything to do with what you bring to talk about. Before you can have a really rich conversation, you've got to notice something significant, something provocative, and then mull it over in your mind, doing some thinking to prepare."

TEACHING

Further explain the teaching point, emphasizing the importance of preparation for book-club conversations.

"If you want to have a so-so book-club conversation, it's pretty easy. You just have to find a few facts you can share or think up a quick summary of what you read. But, to have a really rich conversation, the kind that helps you think more deeply about your reading, you've got to prepare. Specifically, it helps to notice fascinating parts and then to mull those parts over, generating ideas and questions and formulating some thinking about them. You almost need to have a book-club conversation in your mind to prepare for the conversation you'll have with your club later."

Book clubs...

* Meet regularly.

* Come to meetings prepared.

* Talk about the text.

* Reference pages in the book.

* Run their own meetings.

Students at this level won't need a lot of instruction in the basics of book clubs. Even if they haven't had a ton of book-club experience, briefly sharing a chart like this should be a sufficient way to help them get their clubs up and running quickly.

When we write units of study books, we often revise the teaching point scores of times. Wording a teaching point just right is deceptively complex. In this case, we angled the teaching point to very specifically name the steps in the thinking work readers must do to get ready for a book club. The primary goal of the teaching point, then, is to help students get better at reading. Helping them to have better book-club conversations is a secondary goal.

Rally the class to function as a giant book club. Read an excerpt from your read-aloud text, and then pause to model how you notice a fascinating part.

"Let's pretend to be a giant book club and try this with a section a bit further on in *Fast Food Nation*, where we learn about how one of the biggest fast food chains—McDonald's—got its start. We'll read a bit, pushing ourselves to notice fascinating parts that will lead to rich talk.

"The text starts when the McDonald brothers have just one burger bar restaurant, and it's already making them rich. They own a kind of restaurant called a drive-in, where customers parked outside and servers brought food to their cars. Those servers were called carhops. Ready?" I started reading aloud, displaying an image of carhops as I read that part aloud.

> *By the end of the 1940s the McDonald brothers had grown dissatisfied with the drive-in business. They were tired of constantly looking for new carhops and short-order cooks—who were in great demand—as the old ones left for higher-paying jobs elsewhere. They were tired of replacing the dishes, glassware, and silverware their teenage customers constantly broke or ripped off. And they were tired of their teenage customers. The brothers thought about selling the restaurant. Instead, they tried something new.*
>
> *The McDonalds fired all their carhops in 1948, closed their restaurant, installed larger grills, and reopened three months later with a radically new method of preparing food. It was designed to increase the speed, lower prices, and raise the volume of sales. The brothers eliminated almost two-thirds of the items on their old menu. They got rid of everything that had to be eaten with a knife, spoon, or fork. The only sandwiches now sold were hamburgers or cheeseburgers. The brothers got rid of their dishes and glassware, replacing them with paper cups, paper bags, and paper plates. They divided the food preparation into separate tasks performed by different workers. To fill a typical order, one person grilled the hamburger; another "dressed" and wrapped it; another prepared the milk shake; another made the fries; and another worked the counter. For the first time, the guiding principles of a factory assembly line were applied to a commercial kitchen. The new division of labor meant that a worker only had to be taught how to perform one task. Skilled and expensive short-order cooks were no longer necessary. All the burgers were sold with the same condiments: ketchup, onions, mustard, and two pickles. No substitutions were allowed. The McDonald brothers' Speedee Service System revolutionized the restaurant business. An ad of theirs seeking franchises later spelled out the benefits of the system: "Imagine—No Carhops—No Waitresses—No Dishwashers—No Bus Boys—The McDonald's System is Self-Service!"*

"It would be easy to just name some of the facts from this part to each other, right? We could just name all the things that the McDonald brothers did in order, but I don't think our book-club conversation would go anywhere. Instead, let's look for fascinating parts that we think would lead to great talk, and then mull them over, having a book club in our minds to prepare for the conversations we'll have later.

"Watch me try this first, then you'll have a chance. Hmm, . . . What part would I pick?" I skimmed the text, then I said, "How about this: 'They got rid of everything that had to be eaten with a knife, spoon, or fork'? That part jumped out for me, and I think it would make for rich conversation."

If you worry that this text will be challenging for your students, there are a few ways you can make it more comprehensible. You could pre-read the text with students so they encounter it here as a reread. You could use images, or tuck in quick definitions, to convey unfamiliar content, as you do here with carhops. You could also substitute in an easier passage, perhaps using a similar excerpt from Chew On This: Everything You Don't Want to Know About Fast Food *(see the online resources for suggested substitutions).*

Demonstrate how you mull a part over to prepare for conversation, then ask clubs to continue mulling over the part you shared.

"Am I ready to bring this part to our club? Definitely not! Before I bring this idea to our club, I have to mull it over. To mull a part over, it helps to ask questions about it, to try growing some ideas. I'll start mulling this part over, and will you be ready to finish? Well, I hadn't even thought about the fact that McDonald's doesn't use silverware. I'm wondering why they would have decided to get rid of silverware. Let me push myself to consider a few possibilities. Maybe it was because people were breaking and stealing it, like the text mentioned earlier. Or, it could be because they wanted people to be able to eat on the go? Maybe it was part of their 'Speedee Service System'; not only could the food be prepared faster, it could be eaten faster too.

"Will you continue mulling this over in your mind? Try saying, 'Maybe . . . ,' 'Perhaps . . . ,' or 'Could it be . . . ?'"

Debrief, naming the transferable work you just modeled, choosing a fascinating part and mulling it over to prepare for later book-club conversations.

After thirty seconds, I reconvened the class. "Readers, did you see how we prepared for a richer conversation by noticing fascinating parts and then mulling them over? We asked questions and grew ideas about that part. It was almost like we had a book-club conversation in our minds. Now, we're prepared for a more significant conversation."

ACTIVE ENGAGEMENT

Set students up to try the work you modeled. Ask them to reread the text, notice another significant part, and mull it over, asking questions about it and growing ideas.

"Ready to try this on your own? I'll display the chunk of text we just read aloud, and will you look it over and think about a part you could talk a lot off of? Give me a thumbs up when you have something in mind."

I waited until most students had a thumb up, and then I said, "Now that you've got a part, mull it over in your mind. Ask questions about it, consider possible answers, and grow some ideas from that part. Have a book-club conversation in your mind to prepare to talk with your group."

Then, channel one student from each club to share an idea, and coach clubs as they talk.

"One of you in the club, get started by sharing something significant, maybe even something provocative. Say, 'Let me catch you up on my thinking so far . . .' and then share what you've been thinking. Everyone else, be ready to talk long about what your club member shares. See if you can keep growing your thinking about that one part until I call you back together. Remember that if you're not sure about what the perfect response is, you can say things like, 'Maybe it could be . . .' or 'Perhaps it could be . . .'"

While students talked, I coached in with brief tips to help students extend their conversation.

Even if your students have been in book clubs for years, your teaching here will significantly lift the level of their talk. Just a bit of preparation can make the world of difference for students' conversations.

- "Add onto that idea."
- "Tell whether you agree or disagree and why."
- "Ask each other questions."

I called students back to quickly summarize a few of their points. "Wow, you brought really significant, provocative ideas to your club conversations! Some of you noticed the part that said 'skilled and expensive short-order cooks were no longer necessary.' You came ready with questions like, 'Was this new system the McDonald brothers put into place really better?' You made connections, in this case, to restaurants in our community that don't treat teenage customers very well. Then, you talked a ton off those points, pushing yourself by saying, 'Maybe . . .' and 'Could it be . . .' and 'Perhaps . . .' Talking long off those parts really helped make your conversation richer."

LINK

Reference the anchor chart to remind students of the repertoire of work nonfiction readers can do, and then set them up to generate plans for their own reading.

"I think you could talk for the rest of class about these significant ideas and questions you've developed, but I know you're dying to do your own thinking about your book-club books."

I added a new point to our anchor chart. "Most of you already oriented yourself to the text and read all the front matter closely, developing questions and growing initial ideas as you did. Now, you know that having a strong book-club conversation has everything to do about the quality of your conversation. When you notice fascinating parts and mull them over, you come to your conversations prepared with so much to talk about.

> **ANCHOR CHART**
>
> To Make the Most of Your
> Nonfiction Chapter Books . . .
>
> - Orient yourself to the text.
>   - Review the front cover and table of contents.
>   - Read the front matter to spark questions and ideas.
> - **Notice fascinating parts and mull them over to prepare for rich conversations.**

Notice fascinating
parts, and mull them
over.

Flag a page!   ...Perhaps...
               Could it be...
               Maybe...

Jot a few points.

"With your club, make a quick plan for your reading. Decide how many pages you'll read today and if there's anything particular you want to pay attention to as you read. You'll have thirty minutes to read today, so you'll probably read around twenty pages. Keep in mind all you know about making the most of your nonfiction reading as you do. Off you go!"

Lifting the Level of Work through Quick Table Conferences

TODAY, your students will make a plan for their reading with their clubs, identifying how many pages they'll read and if there's anything particular they'll think about as they read. Developing a plan should be quick, so keep the students in the meeting area as they plan and be ready to send them off to read in a minute or two if they have not developed a plan. Expect that students should spend the majority of their time today reading, ideally reading about twenty pages in thirty minutes. As they read, students might note or flag thought-provoking ideas they can later bring to their club conversations.

As is typical anytime you launch a new unit, the first few days are not the ideal time to settle down with a student for a lengthy one-on-one conference or to pull small groups to address targeted skills. Instead, your students need to feel your presence around the room. As you move around the room to work with informal groups of students, you'll be able to use eye contact, gestures, and quick verbal redirections to get all students on track and engaged in the work of the unit.

Table conferences will be particularly effective for helping you meet with a wide range of students. To do a table conference, pull up next to a table of students and observe for a minute. It helps to observe with some predictable tips in mind (see the "If . . . Then . . ." chart that follows). Perhaps you notice that the students at the table are doing a lot of writing about their reading and not a lot of reading, or perhaps you notice a student pick up a new article and dive in without orienting herself to the text. Look for something that you notice multiple students need support with.

Then, you might say, "All eyes up here," and pause the table group to give a quick tip. You'll probably name the tip and then ask students to try it, or you'll give a little explanation of how you do the work yourself as a reader. You won't have time to do a demonstration of these strategies because you'll want to get to all your readers today.

After you give a tip, spend a few minutes coaching the kids at the table as they try out the tip. Use lean prompts, and aim to stay with each student for about thirty seconds or so, just long enough to get that student going on some slightly better work than they were doing independently. For instance, if you're working with a student who is doing too much writing about reading, you might say, "Read for five more pages before you stop," and then move on to the next student. Leave the kids with a quick reminder to practice the work going forward before moving on to the next group.

If you see . . .	Then you can say . . .
Students are reading without expression, despite the variety in the information they are taking in.	"Readers react to the content they're reading. When they read something terrifying or surprising or absolutely entertaining, they have a reaction. They might gasp, make a face, laugh out loud, or even tear up. These reactions help readers stay engaged in the book they're reading. "Get back into your books, and this time, make your face match the reactions in your brain. When you're amused, chuckle. When you're surprised, gasp! Let yourself react to what's happening in the book."

If you see . . .	Then you can say . . .
Students are spending more than 10% of their reading time writing about their reading.	"Most of your reading time should be made up of time where you're actually reading to figure out what the text is teaching. In fact, reading researchers at Columbia University say a good rule of thumb is that you should only spend 10% of your reading time writing about your reading. Today, you're reading for about thirty minutes, so 10% of that would be . . . three minutes! This means you'll have to read for a much longer chunk of time before you stop and jot. "Ready to try this? Get started reading on in your book, pushing yourself to read to the end of a longer section, maybe even a chapter, before you stop to do any jotting."
Students are only reading one part of their books (either the text or the text features) and are not synthesizing across both parts.	"I want to give you a tip: everything on the page, from the title to the text features and captions, is there for a reason. As a reader, you have to take in everything on the page—the words and the text features—to figure out what the text is teaching. To do that, you can read a new part and think, 'How does this fit with what I just read?' "Give this a try. Read on in your books, being sure to read both the words and the text features. When you get to a new part, pause for a moment and ask yourself, 'How does this fit with what I just read?' Try to name how the new part fits with what you already read."
Some club members are waiting for another club member to finish reading a part before reading on.	"To make the most of your reading time, you won't want to just sit around waiting for other people in your club to finish reading a section before you move on. Let me give you some tips for what you can do instead. First, you could go back and reread a part that seems critical or a part that felt confusing. Second, you could do a little bit of writing about the thought-provoking ideas and questions you want to bring to your club conversation. Or third, you could keep reading. You might get a little bit ahead of your club, but that's okay. "Right now, pick up your books. I'm going to admire you as you make a smart choice about what you can do right now as a reader that will help you a lot more than sitting here doing nothing will."
Clubs are spending much of reading time talking.	"To make your book-club conversations super-strong, you need to spend some time reading, so you can generate really thought-provoking ideas, the kind your club will be able to linger with, the kind that might even make you rethink what you are thinking about the text. Doing that kind of dedicated, nose-in-the-book reading first will help you make sure your group can have the strongest conversation possible. "Get right back into your books, and this time, keep our tips about growing thought-provoking ideas in mind. I'm going to coach in as you're reading."

Drawing on All You Know to Hold Powerful Book-Club Conversations

Briefly review what students know about book clubs. Give them a moment to prepare, then invite them to talk in their clubs.

"Readers, it's book-club time. You know what to do: come prepared, talk about the text, reference pages in the book, run your own book-club meeting so that no one person dominates the conversation. And today, you learned that your club conversations will be richer if you do some significant thinking in advance to prepare. Take a minute right now to prepare for your conversation. You might use Post-it notes to flag a page in the text you want to reference, or you might jot down a few points you want to make during your conversation."

A minute later, I channeled the students to get started. "Readers, when you're ready, get started talking!" I moved quickly from club to club, listening in to club conversations. I whispered tips into the ears of a few students such as, "Ask a question," "Tell if you agree or disagree," and "Tell them what page to turn to."

USING THE WHOLE TEXT TO GENERATE CONVERSATION-WORTHY IDEAS

Readers, you know that one hallmark of nonfiction books is text features, such as photos, diagrams, graphs, and tables. As nonfiction books become more sophisticated, often so do the text features. In the kinds of books you're reading now, the text features are rarely there just as decoration. They serve a purpose, and they often teach new information.

As you read tonight, search the text features as well as the text for significant parts that you can bring to your book club. A text feature might lead you to make a connection, or to ask a question that could spark debate. Take a minute or two to record some of your thinking to prepare for your next club conversation.

Determining Central Ideas

GETTING READY

✔ Prepare to add to the "To Make the Most of Your Nonfiction Chapters Books . . ." anchor chart (see Teaching Point).

✔ Display images that belong together in simple and more complex ways: spoon, fork, and knife, then add a salt shaker and plate (see Teaching).

✔ Display images that belong together in a deeper way: animal parents and their own babies: tigers, gorillas, and giraffes (see Teaching).

✔ Select an excerpt from your read-aloud text for students to identify details and analyze how they fit together. We chose pages 53–54 from *Fast Food Nation* (see Active Engagement).

✔ Leave Post-its at students' desks for them to mark possible central ideas (see Link).

✔ Identify a few excerpts from *Fast Food Nation* that you can use to model using a pop-out sentence and headings to determine central ideas (see Conferring and Small-Group Work).

✔ Prepare to add to the "Book Clubs . . ." chart (see Share).

IN THIS SESSION

TODAY YOU'LL remind students that one of a nonfiction reader's main jobs is determining central ideas. You'll review familiar strategies for doing so, and you'll teach readers that another way nonfiction readers determine central ideas is by considering how details fit together.

TODAY YOUR STUDENTS will consider how details fit together to determine central ideas in their nonfiction chapter books as they read.

MINILESSON

CONNECTION

Remind students that nonfiction readers must pay particular attention to central ideas. Invite them to recall strategies they already know for determining central ideas.

"Readers, you know that especially when you're trying to learn everything you can about a topic, it's critical to pay attention to the central ideas—the big points—that the author is making. I know you've learned a ton of strategies that readers can use to determine the central ideas authors are teaching. Will you and your partner quickly list across your fingers some strategies that help you determine central ideas?" I gave students a minute to talk, while I listened in to note the strategies they were familiar with.

I called for the students' attention. "Let me name out some strategies I heard you share. You said sometimes the author comes right out and says the central idea in a pop-out sentence that captures what a big chunk of the text is about. It's usually the first or last sentence in a section, but sometimes it's in the middle. I also heard you say you look to the headings and subheadings to determine central ideas. You said that sometimes, the author pretty much says the central idea in one of the headings.

"Those strategies work sometimes, but as texts get harder, I want to remind you of one more strategy that will be particularly helpful for determining central ideas in longer, more complex texts."

❖ **Name the teaching point.**

"Today I want to remind you that nonfiction readers work hard to determine a text's central ideas. One way they do this is to notice important details in the text and then to look across those details and think, 'How do these details fit together?'"

I encourage you to share out these strategies, even if your students don't mention them. These are two strategies for determining central ideas that are most taught in elementary schools, so it's likely your students have encountered them before. Naming them here will help to jog students' memories.

ANCHOR CHART

To Make the Most of Your
Nonfiction Chapter Books . . .

- Orient yourself to the text.
  - Review the front cover and table of contents.
  - Read the front matter to spark questions and ideas.
- Notice fascinating parts and mull them over to prepare for rich conversations.
- **Determine possible central ideas.**
  - **Use pop-out sentences and headings.**
  - **Locate details across sections and think, "How do these details fit together?**

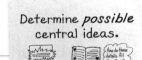

Determine *possible* central ideas.

TEACHING

Quickly share a series of images to help students understand how readers determine possible central ideas by studying the details in the text.

"Let me give you some examples of what I mean. Imagine I found these details in the text." I displayed pictures of a knife, fork, and spoon. "Details like these would fit together in a pretty straightforward way, right? But you, the reader of these pictures, have to invent the words that convey how these fit together. You can't find the big idea in the text itself—in the pictures of these three items. The big idea comes from your mind. It's not hard to generate it, however. If

I asked, 'How do these details fit together?' you'd say, . . ." I gestured for students to respond. They called out, "They're all silverware!" and, "They're all things you eat with."

"Well, in longer texts, it's not always quite so obvious how details fit together. In addition to details like a knife, fork, and spoon, you'll also have details like these." I added a picture of a saltshaker and a plate to the collection. "Again, you have to ask yourself, 'How do these details fit together?' Brainstorm with your partner."'

I gave students thirty seconds to talk, coaching to encourage them to explain how the details fit with the idea they proposed. Then, I gathered them and recapped, "I heard you saying these details could fit together because they're all things you find in a kitchen or they're all things that help you eat dinner."

Set students up to study one more set of images. Encourage them to move beyond the topic to explain how, specifically, the details fit together.

"Let's try one more." I revealed several images of animals. "Now, I know, when I ask you 'How do these details fit together?' it would be really easy to say, 'They're all animals.' Try to push yourself beyond that. How, specifically, do these details fit together? Talk with your partner." Again, I gave students about thirty seconds to talk.

Keep these turn-and-talk intervals brief. Give students thirty seconds to talk, then call them back and summarize. Your goal is to give students some quick, repeated practice determining central ideas.

I called them back together and said, "I agree. When you really study how, specifically, these details fit together, you could say one central idea of these photos is that animal parents take care of their babies. Another idea could be that many young animals resemble their parents, only smaller versions of them."

ACTIVE ENGAGEMENT

Rally students to try the work in a text. Ask them to first collect details that feel important. Then, set them up to consider how the details fit together, so they name a possible central idea for the text.

"The work is similar in a text. Are you ready to try it? We'll read a new part of *Fast Food Nation* today. Remember, it helps to read a section on the lookout for details that seem important. Hold up a finger each time you hear a detail that sounds important." I read the section aloud to students, extending a finger each time I encountered an important detail.

> (S)elling more soda to kids has become one of the easiest ways to meet sales projections. "Influencing elementary school students is very important to soft drink marketers," an article in the January 1999 issue of Beverage Industry *explained, "because children are still establishing their tastes and habits." Eight-year-olds are considered ideal customers; they have about sixty-five years of purchasing in front of them. "Entering the schools makes perfect sense," the trade journal concluded.*
>
> The fast food chains also benefit enormously when children drink more soda. The chicken nuggets, hamburgers, and other main courses sold at fast food restaurants usually have the lowest profit margins. Soda has by far the highest. "We at McDonald's are thankful," a top executive once told the New York Times, "that people like drinks with their sandwiches." Today, McDonald's sells more Coca-Cola than anyone else in the world. The fast food chains purchase Coca-Cola syrup for about $4.25 a gallon. A medium Coke that sells for $1.29 contains roughly 9 cents' worth of syrup. Buying a large Coke for $1.49 instead, as the cute girl behind the counter always suggests, will add another 3 cents' worth of syrup—and another 17 cents in pure profit for McDonald's.

"Share the details you collected with your partner." I listened in while students turned and talked.

If you think this text excerpt will be challenging for your students, remember you can always take two minutes to read it to your students prior to your minilesson, so that they encounter it here as a reread.

After a minute, I called students back and shared some of what I'd overheard. "You've got some key details in mind: influencing elementary-schoolers is really important for the soda companies; eight-year-olds are ideal customers for soda companies; soda companies sell a Coke for $1.29 that only costs them nine cents to make. Those are the specifics like the salt shaker, the plate, the fork.

"Now the question is: how do these details fit together? Work with a partner to determine the central idea the author might be getting at in this section."

While partnerships talked, I voiced over with tips. To one partnership, I said, "Don't just name a topic—drinking soda. Tell what the text might be teaching you about that topic." To another, I said, "Complex texts often teach multiple central ideas. Look across the details for another central idea this text might be hinting at."

Name a central idea you heard students share.

"I heard you saying one central idea could be that fast food companies market their products to kids so they can make more money. You pointed to details like *eight-year-olds are considered ideal customers* and *soda has by far the highest profit margin*. Locating key details and asking, 'How do these details fit together?' pushed you to determine a possible central idea."

LINK

Restate the teaching point, and connect it to the repertoire of ongoing work students should be drawing on as they read.

"To get as smart as you can about the topics you're studying, it's not enough to be fascinated. You also have to grasp what the author is teaching, what the central ideas are in the text. Sometimes a central idea might be taught explicitly, captured in pop-out sentences and headings, but often it is taught implicitly, and you have to locate key details and ask, 'How do these details fit together?' I left sticky notes on your desks that you can use to mark parts where you identify possible central ideas.

"As you read today, remember there's lots of work you can draw on." I referenced the anchor chart. "Be alert to the thought-provoking parts of your text, and also work to develop some initial ideas about what the text is teaching.

"First, make a plan with your club for what you'll read and think about. When your plan is developed, off you go!"

Summarizing students' responses after a turn and talk, rather than calling on students to share, keeps the minilesson brief so students have more time to read. It also ensures students hear a proficient version of the work.

Supporting Foundational Work around a Central Idea

SINCE THE UNIT IS STILL NEW, you'll again want to devote some time to rallying students to the work of the unit. You might spend the first five minutes or so of the workshop leading table conferences to ensure students are orienting to nonfiction texts, reading with engagement, and spending the majority of their time reading instead of writing about their reading. Refer to the "If . . . Then . . ." grid in the Conferring and Small-Group Work section for Session 2 for suggestions about what to look for when observing book clubs and for language you can use when leading these table conferences.

Then, you might shift your focus to the new work you introduced today. One major focus early in this unit will be supporting students in determining central ideas in their texts, so they become true experts on their topics. This work lays the foundation for your upcoming teaching. Across the next two bends, you'll build upon this skill as you teach students to revise their understanding of a central idea as they read, to consider text structure when determining central ideas, and to summarize, creating a concise version of the text.

Moving from a Topic to a Central Idea

Take a minute to look across the quick jots your students are making as they read, or talk to a few students about what their texts are teaching. You'll probably find some students are only naming topics. For instance, when reading the introduction to *Fast Food Nation*, they say that the text is teaching about "fast food," "food delivery," or "air force stations." The next step for these students is to consider not just the topic, but what the book aims to teach about the topic. In this way, they move closer to determining the text's central ideas.

Gather these students together for a small group to teach them that moving from naming a topic to naming a central idea usually means a shift from a noun phrase to a sentence. You might begin by telling students why you gathered them and stating the teaching point. "I'm noticing it's easy for you to name the topic of your text, the big

general thing the text is teaching about. What I want to teach you is that to really learn from a text and become an expert, you've got to think, 'What is the author teaching me about this topic?' That can help you to name a possible central idea."

Then, you could refer to your read-aloud text to share an example of how readers move from a topic to a possible central idea. "Remember how I did this with the introduction? I first noticed that the whole section was about fast food. That was the topic. Then I asked myself, 'What is the author teaching me about this topic?' That led me to a possible big idea: fast food can be found everywhere, even where you don't expect it. Do you see how I moved from naming a topic to naming a central idea?"

Then, set students up to practice the work. You might say, "Will you give this a try? Read a section of your text and then pause, and push yourself to think, 'What is the author teaching me about this topic?' Try to say or write what the author is teaching in a sentence. This could be a possible central idea. Try this with one section, and then read and try it with another section."

The goal is that students will approximate this work, doing slightly better work than before. Once all students are started, spend a few minutes coaching in, moving from kid to kid as you give lean tips: "What might be the central idea of this section?"; "That's the topic. What's the author teaching you about that topic?"; "Look for a few pieces of evidence to back up that idea"; or "Read on, on the lookout for other big ideas the text might be teaching." Leave the group with a reminder to continue practicing this work.

Determining Central Ideas When Stated Explicitly

Other students might need support determining central ideas that are stated explicitly in the text. They might have trouble identifying pop-out sentences or using the heading to determine a central idea. These are strategies you reminded students of in the mini-lesson but did not teach in depth. You could lead small groups teaching either strategy.

If students need support identifying pop-out sentences, you might gather them and say, "Sometimes, the central idea is captured in a pop-out sentence, a sentence that almost pops out of the page when you read because it seems so important. This is usually the first or last sentence in a paragraph, but not always. To determine if there's a pop-out sentence, you can identify a sentence that *seems* important and then check the other sentences in the paragraph or section to see if they fit with the potential pop-out sentence."

You could use the first paragraph of "What We Eat" from the introduction of *Fast Food Nation* to model determining a pop-out sentence. After noticing that the first sentence functions as a pop-out sentence, you could check it against the other sentences, asking, "Do these details fit with that pop-out sentence?" Then, give students a chance to read their books while you coach in, alert for central ideas that might be taught in pop-out sentences.

You might gather another group of students to support them in using headings or chapter titles to determine the central ideas. Name your teaching point: "Nonfiction readers work hard to determine central ideas in their texts, so they can really become experts. One strategy that sometimes helps is to study the headings and chapter titles and ask, 'What is the text teaching me about this heading?'" You might explain that sometimes headings can be misleading or use figurative language that throws readers off, but other times they are fairly straightforward.

You could reference a couple of sections from *Fast Food Nation* as examples, especially "the founding fathers" (p. 14), "speedee service" (p. 18), and "kid kustomers" (p. 43). Quickly show students how you study these headings and the following text to determine central ideas. Then, get them started practicing this work in their own books while you coach in.

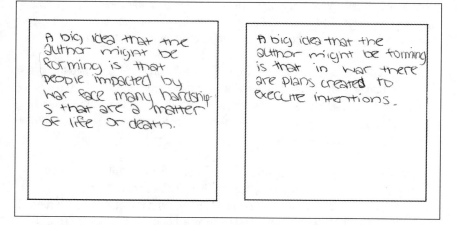

FIG. 3–1 Caitlin jots possible central ideas from the first few chapters of her book on Post-it notes.

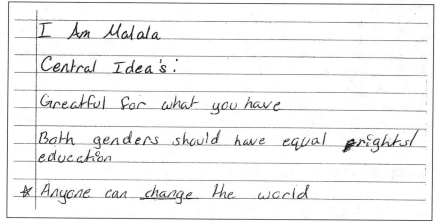

FIG. 3–2 Jade uses her reader's notebook to record possible central ideas, and she marks the central idea that is most taught in her book so far with a star.

Setting Ambitious Reading Goals

Explain that book-club members hold one another accountable for meeting goals. Encourage clubs to discuss their reading volume and to brainstorm ways to support one another with reading more.

"Readers, I want to add on one more thing that book clubs do when they meet to our chart. Book-club members hold each other accountable. One of the surefire ways to become a better reader is to read a lot, which means that each of you should be reading around twenty pages in school each day *and* another twenty pages at home. That totals at least forty pages of reading a day."

"When your club meets in a minute, will you check in about the volume of reading you've already done? Study your reading logs. Did your club read close to twenty pages in school today? At home last night? If not, spend part of your time brainstorming what you can do to support each other. Do you need to stay more focused while reading in school? Do you need to do less jotting? Do you need someone to text you so you remember to read your book tonight?"

"Or, if your club is already meeting that volume goal, brainstorm what you could do to read even more. Maybe you could be reading around the text, that is, finding articles, images, and video clips on the topic and studying those to help you learn more about the topic."

Transition students to conversations with their book clubs.

"Get started talking with your book club, and be sure to spend at least a few minutes discussing your reading volume and ways you can support one another."

Book clubs...

* *Meet regularly.*

* *Come to meetings prepared.*

* *Talk about the text.*

* *Reference pages in the book.*

* *Run their own meetings.*

* *Hold each other accountable.*

SESSION 3 HOMEWORK

DETERMINING CENTRAL IDEAS

As you read tonight, stay on the lookout for your book's central ideas and pay attention to the methods you use to find them. In some books, the headings lead straight to central ideas. In others, the central ideas are more hidden, and you might have to try other methods, like looking closely at how details fit together. Take a few minutes and jot about the central ideas you find. Tomorrow, you'll report central ideas to your club, along with the methods that worked best for you to find them.

Rethinking Initial Ideas

GETTING READY

✔ Prepare to show the animal images from Session 3, along with three new photos that introduce new information (see Teaching).

✔ Select an excerpt from your read-aloud text that would lead students to rethink their initial central idea. We chose pages 72–73 from *Fast Food Nation* (see Active Engagement).

✔ Prepare to add to the anchor chart, "To Make the Most of Your Nonfiction Chapter Books . . ." (see Link).

✔ Print reminder slips you can leave behind after table conferences and small groups (see Conferring and Small-Group Work).

✔ Prepare to show note-taking methods that capture thinking about central ideas (see Share).

IN THIS SESSION

TODAY YOU'LL teach readers that in complex nonfiction, central ideas are revealed over time. Readers generate initial ideas about what a text teaches, and then revise them as they get more information.

TODAY YOUR STUDENTS will read on with their central ideas in mind, alert for details that might lead them to rethink their initial ideas.

MINILESSON

CONNECTION

This connection references work from A Deep Study of Character. *If you chose to launch the year another way or are teaching this unit in your content-area classroom, you'll want to revise accordingly. You might choose instead to reference a movie or TV show where your thinking about a character changed over time.*

Connect students' earlier work—revising their thinking about characters across a fiction text—to the work nonfiction readers do when they read longer chapter books.

"Readers, remember a few weeks ago when we did a deep study of the characters in our books? We realized that our initial ideas about the characters were insufficient, since our characters tended to reveal themselves over time. Our first ideas didn't take the whole character into account. To develop truly accurate ideas about our characters, we had to read alert to new details, ready to rethink our initial ideas.

"Well, the same is true for the longer nonfiction chapter books you're reading."

♣ **Name the teaching point.**

"Today I want to teach you that in complicated nonfiction books, just like in complicated stories, central ideas only reveal themselves over time. Experienced readers, therefore, are alert to new details, and they rethink their first ideas in light of new evidence."

TEACHING

Revisit yesterday's work around determining central ideas. Show students how you revise your thinking about a central idea after noticing new details.

"Let's try this. Yesterday, we studied some images of animals with their babies, and you said one central idea might be that animal parents take care of their babies. Imagine that we read on in that same text, alert for new details that might somehow fit with that central idea, and we came across these additional details." I revealed the images students studied yesterday alongside three new photos.

"The central idea we generated yesterday—that animal parents take care of their babies—isn't really enough anymore if we take these new pictures into account. We could just jot down another central idea, but in books like these, the central ideas tend to be revealed slowly, so rather than come up with one new idea after the next, often we have to rethink our initial ideas to come up with an idea that takes into account the whole text.

"Try it with your partner. What do these new details suggest? How could you revise the central idea to incorporate all these new details?"

I gave students a minute to talk, and then called them together. "I was thinking the same thing. These new details aren't of a parent caring for their own baby. Instead, they show animals caring for babies who are *not* their own. So maybe a revised central idea could be that some animals have natural nurturing instincts. They are willing to care for animals who are not even in their own species."

Debrief, naming the transferable strategy.

"Do you see how, just like in the complicated stories we read earlier in the year, central ideas often reveal themselves over time? We had to hold our initial ideas loosely and rethink them in light of the new details in the text."

At the end of your teaching, it's powerful to restate the strategy you just modeled using transferrable language, so students have another chance to hear it.

ACTIVE ENGAGEMENT

Set students up to try this work with a section of the read-aloud text. Challenge students to listen for details that would lead them to rethink their initial thoughts about the central ideas.

"Readers, ready to try this work with *Fast Food Nation*? Yesterday we jotted a possible central idea from *Fast Food Nation*—that fast food companies market to kids to make more money. Since this text is more complicated, we'll have to hold that initial idea loosely, and read on alert to new details in the text that might make us rethink our initial idea." I read aloud an excerpt from pages 72–73.

> The nation has about 1 million migrant farm workers and about 3.5 million fast food workers. Although picking strawberries is orders of magnitude more difficult than cooking hamburgers, both jobs are now filled by people who are generally young, unskilled, and willing to work long hours for low pay. Moreover, the turnover rates for both jobs are among the highest in the American economy. The annual turnover rate in the fast food industry is now about 300 to 400 percent. The typical fast food worker quits or is fired every three to four months.
>
> The fast food industry pays the minimum wage to a higher proportion of its workers than any other American industry. Consequently, a low minimum wage has long been a crucial part of the fast food industry's business plan.

"Instead of jotting down a brand-new idea, let this information lead you to rethink the central idea you've tentatively identified. And don't just say if a detail fits. Explain *how* the detail fits. Quick, tell your partner what you're thinking."

I gave students a few minutes to talk, while I voiced over with tips:

* "This book will only teach a few central ideas. Instead of jotting another one, try rethinking your initial idea. How could you revise that idea to include this new information?"

* "Point to specific details from the text that give you that idea."

* "Make sure your revised big idea fits both what we just read and what we read before."

Summarize how students suggested that they could revise the central idea to incorporate the new information.

I gathered the class back together and said, "I heard you saying that the details in this part show that fast food companies are taking advantage of people who really need jobs by not paying them well and then fighting to pay them even less. Instead of jotting that as a second central idea, you considered how this new information could fit with the central idea you already had: that fast food companies market to kids to make money. These new details helped you revise that idea. So a central idea might be that fast food companies take advantage of people to make money, whether it's kids or low-income workers."

If you think your students will be unfamiliar with a concept, such as minimum wage, resist the urge to pause your lesson to teaching into it here. Instead, tuck in a brief, one-sentence definition, and then continue reading.

LINK

Restate the teaching point, and add the new work to the anchor chart. Encourage clubs to make a quick plan for the work they'll do as readers and then to get started reading.

"Readers, whenever you're reading complicated nonfiction books, hold your initial ideas about what the text teaches loosely. The central ideas will be revealed over time. As you read, remain alert to new details, and be willing to rethink your first ideas in light of new evidence. That kind of careful work will help you understand what the text is *really* teaching." I added this new idea to our anchor chart.

ANCHOR CHART

> To Make the Most of Your
> Nonfiction Chapter Books . . .
>
> - Orient yourself to the text.
>   - Review the front cover and table of contents.
>   - Read the front matter to spark questions and ideas.
> - Notice fascinating parts and mull them over to prepare for rich conversations.
> - Determine possible central ideas.
>   - Use pop-out sentences and headings.
>   - Locate details across sections and think, "How do these details fit together?"
> - **Rethink central ideas in light of new evidence.**

Rethink central ideas in light of new information.

"Before you head off to read today, make a plan with your club. About how many pages will you read in the next thirty minutes? Probably around twenty. What kind of reading work will pay off for you? When you've got a plan, head off to get started."

Strengthening Students' Literal Comprehension

AS YOUR STUDENTS HEAD OFF TO READ, take a few moments to survey your class. Look for book clubs to be quickly developing a plan for their work and then spending the majority of their time reading. Scan students' reading logs to make sure the are reading at least forty pages of text a day, including about twenty pages in school and another twenty pages at home. Students' writing about reading will need to be limited in order for them to reach this goal.

You'll probably find some students in your class who will benefit from conferences and small-group work to strengthen their literal comprehension. These might be students who are reading significantly below grade level or who are disengaged readers. These could also be students who are strong fiction readers and feel less confident as readers of nonfiction. These could even be students who are confident readers of easier nonfiction texts and have recently moved to slightly harder nonfiction texts. You might have a club of students with a common need, or you might pull students from different book clubs who need similar instruction into a small group.

The suggestions on the next page will be particularly supportive if your students need work with envisioning, monitoring for sense, or reading fluently. The tips that you can leave behind with students can be printed from the online resources.

If you notice . . .	Then you might teach . . .	Leave readers with . . .

A student is disengaged in their reading and seems to be flipping pages without taking the text in	"Nonfiction readers envision in their minds as they read, just the way fiction readers do. Sometimes, the text almost reads like a fiction story, and they make a mental movie in their minds. "Other times, the author teaches a lot of information, and readers make boxes and bullets, or timelines, or diagrams in their minds.
	
	"Ready to try it? Start reading and work to envision as you read. Notice whether the text sounds like a story or sounds like it's teaching information, and envision accordingly. I'll coach you as you work."
		Nonfiction readers envision:
		• Sounds like a story?
		  • Mental movie
		• Sounds like teaching information?
		  • Boxes and bullets
		  • Timelines
		  • Diagrams

A student is having trouble retelling what happened in a text or naming a central idea	"Readers expect the nonfiction texts they're reading will make sense. When the text stops making sense—when you can't retell it or name the central ideas—you've got to do something. It helps to reread, sketch what's happening, or talk to a partner. "Will you give this a try? Pick up your text and keep reading. Chances are, most of it will make sense. You can stop from time to time to try naming the central ideas. If things stop making sense, turn to one of our strategies to help you."	**When the text stops making sense, do something!** • Reread • Sketch what's happening • Talk to a partner
A student's oral reading sounds choppy, and/or the student is reading in short phrases	"Whenever you read, whether you're reading nonfiction or fiction, you want to read your text as smoothly as possible. Right now, you're reading in phrases that are about three words long. To make your reading sound even smoother, you can scoop up bigger chunks of words, reading four or five or maybe even more words all at once. "Let me show you what I mean." Quickly model how you read two sentences or so of text in small chunks (matching the number of words per chunk the child is currently producing), and then show how you reread that same section of text, reading more words in a chunk so your reading sounds smoother. "Ready to try this? Get started reading aloud, scooping up as many words as you can at once. Try it again and again, until it starts to feel natural to scoop up more words at once."	**Scoop up more words!** **Goal:** _____ words per chunk
A student is not attending to punctuation in meaningful ways	"Nonfiction readers pay particular attention to punctuation because the punctuation often gives subtle clues as to how to read a text. This is particularly true when the sentences are longer. In longer sentences, you have to adjust your voice to show that some parts of the sentence are meant to be subordinate, or less important. To figure this out, it helps to ask, 'How does this part want to be read?' "Try this as you read on in your article. When you get to a complicated sentence, ask yourself, 'How does this part want to be read?' and then try reading it in your head in a way that shows which parts are most important. I'll come around and coach you as you read. Get to it!"	**To read tricky sentences . . .** • Ask, "How does this part want to be read?"

Capturing Thinking about Central Ideas in Book Clubs

Transition students to conversations about their book-club books. Remind them that they are in charge of running their book-club conversations.

"Readers, right now, you have some time at the end of class to meet with your clubs. Remember, you're responsible for running your own book-club conversation. Look at our chart of what nonfiction readers do to make the most of their books, think about how you want to start your conversation, and then get started talking and growing ideas about your books."

Convene students, and remind them of different systems readers can use to jot about central ideas in the text. Encourage them to find a system that works for them.

After about seven minutes, I called students back together.

"When you revise your thinking regularly, it can be tricky to remember precisely what central ideas your book teaches, so it helps to jot them down. Let me give you some tips for how you can do that. Think about which of these strategies will work best for you.

"If you're reading a book that belongs to the school, you could jot your central ideas on Post-it notes or set up pages in your reader's notebook to track how your thinking changes. You'll probably jot using boxes and bullets, though your boxes and your bullets will get revised over time." I displayed a sample.

"If you're reading a copy of the book that's yours to mark up, then you can mark up key details and jot about possible central ideas right in the margins of the page, wherever you find a bit of room." I displayed a sample.

"If you're reading a digital copy of the text, you've got to decide whether you want to take notes digitally or in your notebook.

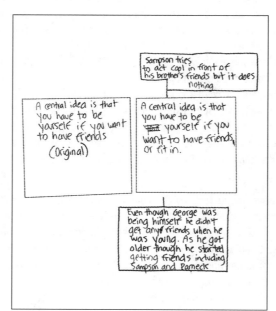

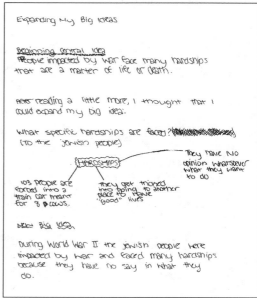

FIG. 4–1   Alex and Molly use different techniques to revise their thinking about their central ideas as they read.

Some people like to use the digital annotation tools, and others prefer paper-and-pencil notes so they can see their notes and the text at the same time.

"Will you talk briefly with your club about the strategy that will work best for you?"

DEVELOPING NOTE-TAKING SYSTEMS

In class today, you studied some note-taking samples and identified a note-taking strategy you thought would work well for you. Let me give you a few more tips to help you make your note-taking as powerful as possible:

- Note-taking should only take 10% of your reading time (or less). That means if you read forty minutes tonight, you should only spend *four* minutes jotting notes, no more.

- Note-taking should be brief. Use abbreviations. Jot in incomplete sentences. Your notes should be much, much shorter than the book you are reading!

- Information you jot down should be *essential*. It will often tie in to the central ideas in the text.

- Note-taking should prepare you for talk. Jot things you want to talk about later with your club.

As you read tonight, will you set aside three or four minutes of your reading time to jot some powerful notes? Remember that most of your time should be spent reading, so you'll still get through twenty-five to thirty pages in your book.

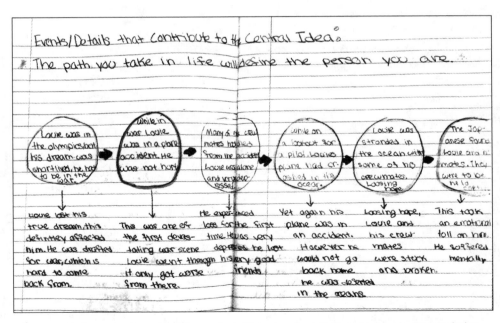

FIG. 4–2   Hailee experiments with a note-taking structure that resembles her central idea by creating a path of events that link to one of her text's central ideas.

Learning from the Stories Embedded in Nonfiction Texts

GETTING READY

✔ Select an excerpt from your read-aloud text for students to consider how the story fits with the central ideas in the text. We chose pages 67–68 from *Fast Food Nation* (see Teaching and Active Engagement).

✔ Write the central idea developed in the previous session on a piece of chart paper or display with a document camera; be prepared to add to it (see Teaching and Active Engagement).

✔ Prepare to add to the "To Make the Most of Your Nonfiction Chapter Books . . ." anchor chart (see Link).

✔ For more advice about running smooth book clubs, refer to the section on book clubs in *A Guide to the Reading Workshop: Middle School Grades* prior to this session.

IN THIS SESSION

TODAY YOU'LL teach students that nonfiction readers pay particular attention to the stories embedded in their texts, considering how those stories fit with the author's central ideas.

TODAY YOUR STUDENTS will read on in their books, considering how embedded stories contribute to central ideas. They'll meet in their clubs, aiming to lift the level of their talk. At the end of the session, they'll make plans to read other texts on their book's topic.

MINILESSON

CONNECTION

Explain that most of the nonfiction books students are reading are filled with stories. Rally students to pay particular attention to what they can learn from those stories embedded in their texts.

"As I've been conferring with you lately, one of the things I've noticed is that your books are just loaded with stories. It will seem like your book is teaching a bunch of facts about the topic and then all of a sudden there's a story. Sometimes the story is about someone famous, like the man who tried to share U.S. nuclear secrets with Russia. Others are about people we've never heard of, like the man who opened a Domino's restaurant and barely made enough money to survive. I get the sense that sometimes you read those stories, think, 'Huh, that's interesting,' or 'Wow! That person is incredibly brave,' and then you power on in the book to the parts that feel like they're teaching you more directly.

"Well, Russell Freedman, a nonfiction author based out of New York City, once said, 'A nonfiction writer is a storyteller who has taken an oath to tell the truth.' Stories are a major way nonfiction writers get across the true information of their topic. What that means is that paying attention to the stories authors embed really matters."

✤ **Name the teaching point.**

"Today I want to teach you that nonfiction readers know that authors embed stories for a reason. Nonfiction readers therefore pay careful attention to the stories to determine how they carry an author's central ideas."

TEACHING AND ACTIVE ENGAGEMENT

Read aloud an excerpt of a story from the class text, then invite students to consider how the story fits with the central ideas in the text.

"Let's try this out together. I was reading more of *Fast Food Nation* last night, and I came across a story that started off a section called 'throughput,' whatever that means. Will you help me read this section, alert to how this story could carry some of the central ideas in the text? One central idea we already generated was that fast food companies take advantage of people to make money, whether it's kids or low-income workers." I began to read aloud from pages 67–68.

> *Every Saturday Elisa Zamot gets up at 5:15 in the morning. It's a struggle, and her head feels groggy as she steps into the shower. Her little sisters, Cookie and Sabrina, are fast asleep in their beds. By 5:30, Elisa's showered, done her hair, and put on her McDonald's uniform. She's sixteen, bright-eyed and olive-skinned, pretty and petite, ready for another day of work. Elisa's mother usually drives her the half-mile or so to the restaurant, but sometimes Elisa walks, leaving home before the sun rises. Her family's modest townhouse sits beside a busy highway on the south side of Colorado Springs, in a largely poor and working-class neighborhood. Throughout the day, sounds of traffic fill the house, the steady whoosh of passing cars. But when Elisa heads for work, the streets are quiet, the sky's still dark, and the lights are out in the small houses and rental apartments along the road.*

"Okay, so we know these stories are here to teach us. Turn and tell your partner what you're already learning from this story."

As I listened to partners talking, I heard many students talking about the anecdote they'd just heard as they would talk about a fictional text. Some were describing Elisa or naming her traits, such as, "she is determined." That was a reasonable response to the passage, but I wanted to be sure they were approaching the text with the lens of "what is this teaching me about fast food restaurants?" so I paused them to offer a tip.

"Readers, here's a tip: the stories in your nonfiction books are fascinating, and it's easy to get lost in them. But it's important to remember that the stories are also teaching information. Instead of saying that Elisa is determined, push yourself to consider what this story might be teaching you."

This time, I heard students sharing that fast food jobs might start early in the morning, even before the sun rises, and that teenagers might work at fast food restaurants.

Read on in the text, encouraging students to continue to be alert to what the text is teaching. Then, channel partnerships to share information the story is teaching.

I gave students about a minute to talk and then said, "Let's read on. We'll keep considering what this story might be teaching us."

> When Elisa arrives at McDonald's, the manager unlocks the door and lets her in. Sometimes the husband-and-wife cleaning crew are just finishing up. More often, it's just Elisa and the manager in the restaurant, surrounded by an empty parking lot. For the next hour or so, the two of them get everything ready. They turn on the ovens and grills. They go downstairs into the basement and get food and supplies for the morning shift. They get the paper cups, wrappers, cardboard containers, and packages of condiments. They step into the big freezer and get the frozen bacon, the frozen pancakes, and the frozen cinnamon rolls. They get the frozen hash browns, the frozen biscuits, the frozen McMuffins. They get the cartons of scrambled egg mix and orange juice mix. They bring the food upstairs and start preparing it before any customers appear, thawing some things in the microwave and cooking other things on the grill. They put the cooked food in special cabinets to keep it warm.
>
> The restaurant opens for business at seven o'clock, and for the next hour or so, Elisa and the manager hold down the fort, handling all the orders. As the place starts to get busy, other employees arrive. Elisa works behind the counter. She takes orders and hands food to customers from breakfast through lunch. When she finally walks home, after seven hours of standing at a cash register, her feet hurt. She's wiped out. She comes through the front door, flops onto the living room couch, and turns on the TV. And the next morning she gets up at 5:15 again and starts the same routine.

"Remember what Russell Freedman said. 'A nonfiction writer is just a storyteller who has taken an oath to tell the truth.' What's Eric Schlosser teaching you here? Tell your partner."

Partners shared with each other more of what they learned from the story about Elisa: a lot of fast food is frozen; cooking fast food is more about reheating food than cooking it from scratch; some people work through the night cleaning fast food restaurants; working at a fast food job can be physically exhausting.

When you say to students, "Let's read on. We'll keep considering what this story might be teaching us," you set a purpose for their listening. This brief set up helps students to see more in a text than they would have otherwise. Look for opportunities to say, "Listen up for . . ." to your students before you read aloud or demonstrate.

When you weave in quotes by authors, you help your students feel as if they are part of a larger community of readers and writers.

Pause students to suggest ways students can connect the work they are doing to the big work of the bend, finding central ideas.

"I want to remind you that astute readers consider how stories might connect to the central ideas of a text. Will you and your partner consider how this story might connect to the central idea we revised yesterday—that fast food companies take advantage of people to make money, whether it's kids or low-income workers? Or, might it be introducing a new central idea?" I projected the central idea jotted on a piece of paper for kids to refer to as they talked.

Possible Central Ideas:

- Fast food companies take advantage of people to make money.

After about three minutes, I called the class back together to debrief. "One partnership said this section was evidence for our central idea, that fast food companies take advantage of people to make money, because it seems like they're working Elisa really hard. And they said it might also help illustrate a new central idea: that fast food is prepared differently than other foods. Do you agree? Let's jot that down as another possible central idea."

You'll return to these notes and revise them in subsequent sessions, which will be easiest if the wording of your notes is similar to the wording here. These notes are intentionally vague so you can strengthen them later.

Possible Central Ideas:

- Fast food companies take advantage of people to make money.
- Fast food is prepared differently than other foods.

Name the work students just did in transferable language.

"Did you see how we approached a story embedded in our nonfiction text differently than a fiction reader would, trying to learn all we could from it? We noticed what the story was teaching, and we considered how it could fit with the central ideas in the text. This led us to discover another possible central idea in the text."

LINK

Restate the teaching point. If students have finished their books, explain that they can get a new text to read. Send students off to make a plan for their work today and then get started.

"In the books you're reading now, there might be a dominant story that comes up throughout the book or small excerpts of stories that pop up from time to time. Either way, pay careful attention to those stories because authors embed them in the text for a reason. Often, they help to illustrate the central ideas in the text." I added a new bullet point to our anchor chart.

To Make the Most of Your
Nonfiction Chapter Books . . .

- Orient yourself to the text.
  - Review the front cover and table of contents.
  - Read the front matter to spark questions and ideas.
- Notice fascinating parts and mull them over to prepare for rich conversations.
- Determine possible central ideas.
  - Use pop-out sentences and headings.
  - Locate details across sections and think, "How do these details fit together?"
- Rethink central ideas in light of new evidence.
- **Consider how embedded stories connect to central ideas.**

Consider how embedded stories connect to central ideas.

"If your club has already finished your book-club book and needs a new one, stay in the meeting area for a minute, so I can help you choose a new book. Otherwise, head off, use our anchor chart to help you decide what you need to work on today, and get started reading!"

Supporting Book Clubs with a Repertoire of Work

TODAY, AS ON MOST TYPICAL DAYS, your students will head off after the minilesson to read independently. Often, they will read their book-club books, and will grow ideas in preparation for their club meetings. At times, some students will have already finished their book-club reading, and rather than read ahead in their club books, they'll choose a different book. Ideally, this will be another nonfiction book in which they can practice the strategies you're teaching. Or, they might read short texts on the same topic as their book-club book, as discussed later in this session. If students have thirty minutes to read, look for them to be reading about twenty pages in their books.

After they've had some time to read on their own, you'll use the share portion of the workshop to channel your students to meet in their book clubs. Following are tips to support students both as they read and as they talk.

Supporting Book Clubs as They Read

Although your students are grouped roughly by reading level and are in clubs with others reading the same book, you will probably find that students within a club have differing needs. For instance, you might notice a handful of students who view each new part of the text as introducing a new central idea, rather than synthesizing information across the text to determine a few big ideas. You might notice students who disregard information that doesn't perfectly fit with their thoughts about a text's central ideas, and you'll need to teach those students to consider how the new information they encounter might lead them to revise their understanding of the text's central ideas. Other students might still be jotting constantly and need to work on significantly limiting their writing about reading so their volume of reading remains high. If this is the case, you'll want to use the time while students are reading to work with students one-on-one through conferences and in strategy groups.

As you did earlier, you might decide to gather small groups of students from across book clubs who share a typical need. Of course, if all students in a club have the same

need, you could meet with that club as a group to teach a strategy. The benefit of this is that clubmates can help keep each other accountable to practicing the work taught in the strategy group.

Look to the conferring and small-group work sections in Sessions 2, 3, and 4 for ideas of small groups you could lead today.

Supporting Book Clubs as They Talk

In addition to supporting students as they read, you'll also want to support book clubs as they discuss the text and their ideas about it. You'll especially want to make sure that students transfer all they know about working with a same-book partner to working in book clubs. When coaching book clubs, avoid jumping into the conversation and leading the conversation for the kids. Book clubs are designed to be student-led, and when you jump in right away, you reduce student autonomy. Be sure to refer to the section on book clubs in *A Guide to the Reading Workshop: Middle School Grades* for more advice on how to ensure book clubs are running as smoothly as possible.

As you listen to book clubs talk, it helps to keep a list of possible teaching focuses in mind. For instance, you might notice clubs that need support with:

- Talking long about one idea for an extended period of time
- Referencing and reading excerpts from the text as they talk
- Using phrases such as "I agree . . ." to add onto the conversation instead of introducing new ideas
- Inviting quieter voices into the conversation
- Asking questions to clarify confusions
- Disagreeing respectfully
- Referencing writing about reading to deepen the conversation

- Making decisions about what's worth discussing as a book club

- Growing ideas through talk so the club walks away with a deeper understanding of the big ideas in the book

We recommend you spend most of your time observing and coaching from outside the book-club circle, using the following repertoire of coaching methods to support your book clubs.

Method of Teaching	Example of How It Could Go
Whisper In The teacher whispers into the ear of a student, suggesting questions the students could ask or sharing tips. The teacher's voice is not heard in the club. conversation.	**Prompt kids to ask a question.** • "Ask him, 'Can you add on?'" • "Say, 'What in the text made you say that?'" • "Ask her if she agrees or disagrees and why." • "Ask him, 'What do you think about that point?'" • "Say, 'What's your evidence for that?'" **Whisper in a tip.** • "Ask a question to invite a quieter voice into the conversation." • "Find evidence in the text for what you're saying." • "Remind everyone to turn to the page you referenced."
Proficient Partner The teacher becomes a club member, joining the conversation briefly to model a specific teaching point. The teacher pauses the club to name the teaching point and then leaves students to continue the conversation independently.	**Explain your role and tell students what to watch for as you coach.** • "I'm going to join your club for two minutes. Will you watch how I ask questions to get the students in your club to say more about their ideas?" **Model what you would like students to try.** • "Can you say more about what you mean?" • "What led you to that idea?" • "What in the text makes you think that?" **Restate what you just taught, and rally students to try the work.** • "Did you see how I asked questions to get the kids in your club to say more about their ideas? Right now, I'm going to leave your club conversation, and will you get started trying this?"
Research-Decide-Teach The teacher observes a club from outside, identifies one teaching point the club could benefit from, and then pauses the club to teach students that one thing.	**Research the club to determine what to teach.** • Ask questions: "What are you working on as a club? How's it going? What's been hard for you that I could help with?" • Observe to determine what students are approximating that you could teach them to do better. **Teach the club one thing.** • "Today I want to teach you that the strongest conversations move beyond saying, 'I agree . . .' Sometimes, clubmates actually disagree with each other, and they express their disagreement by saying, 'I disagree because . . .' or 'I thought something different . . .' or 'I agree with *part* of what you're saying.'" **Demonstrate and/or coach the club as they try the teaching point.** • "I'm going to admire how you try this. Right now, will you pick up where you left off in your conversation? And this time, instead of just saying, 'I agree . . .' to everything, think critically about what your clubmates are saying. If you disagree, tell them so, politely."

Fascinated Readers Read All about a Topic

Explain that when nonfiction readers become fascinated by a topic, they read all they can on that topic. Challenge students to generate a brief list of texts they could read related to their topic.

I called for the class's attention, and asked that students get into their book-club groups. "Readers, you'll have about ten minutes to talk with your clubs today. But before you launch into your conversations, I want to share something with you. It's pretty remarkable how when you start reading a whole book about a topic, especially a book filled with true stories, you get fascinated by that topic, even if you weren't that interested in the topic before. How many of you have had that happen with your book? When I started reading *Fast Food Nation*, for instance, I became fascinated by fast food, even though I rarely eat it, because the stories about people whose real lives were affected by the industry totally hooked me.

"Readers who are fascinated tend to read all about a topic. They'll find articles that relate to the topic, watch YouTube videos, listen to podcasts, pore over documentaries, and more. Last night, I started doing this with our topic, fast food. I found this documentary, *Supersize Me*, which looks at some of the horrible effects too much fast food can have on the human body. And, I found an article about how fast food is as unhealthy as ever, despite all the salads that are getting added to menus."

Shift students into book-club conversations. Suggest that they brainstorm ways to learn more about their topics at the start of their conversations.

"What do you think you could read tonight that relates to your topic? What could you watch? Search for online? Use the first few minutes of your club conversation to brainstorm a brief list of where you could look to find more about your topic. Then, launch into deeper conversations about your books."

SESSION 5 HOMEWORK

 ## READING ON AND ALL ABOUT YOUR TOPIC

Readers, tonight extend your research. Return to the list you started at the end of class, and choose a couple of sources on your topic to check out. You might read an article online or search for a YouTube video that might shed some new light. Then, return to your book, taking this information into account. Make sure you jot for three or four minutes about some of your new thinking.

Ideas Have Roots

Tracing How Ideas Are Developed across a Text

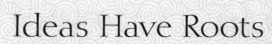

IN THIS SESSION

TODAY YOU'LL teach students that readers pay attention to ideas, events, and people in a text that initially seem insignificant, aware they might be linked to central ideas in the text.

TODAY YOUR STUDENTS will consider how seemingly insignificant parts connect to the bigger ideas in a text as they read. They will analyze their writing about reading with their clubs at the end of the session.

MINILESSON

CONNECTION

Share an image with students to set up the session's teaching.

"Readers, I want to give you some feedback. I'm noticing that a lot of you are talking about this or that part of the text as if it isn't part of the larger text. You sort of put blinders on and talk about an event or an idea that comes up on, say, page 62, and you don't talk about how that event or that idea threads through the whole text. That is, I hear you talking about just the most recent place in the book where that idea or that person crops up and not about the backdrop.

"Have you seen photos of mangrove trees in Florida?" I displayed a picture of the mangrove's root system. "The cool thing about the mangrove is that you can take a tiny little tree stalk and pull on it, and you'll find that even the tiniest tree, one that seems like not much on its own, is often rooted into this giant elaborate web of interconnected roots. It's a lot like the books you're reading now. Even small parts of the book can be connected to ideas that are much bigger."

❖ **Name the teaching point.**

"Today I want to teach you that nonfiction readers know that even ideas, events, and people that initially might seem insignificant are often linked to central ideas in the text. One way to think about this is by asking, 'How might this part fit with what came before?'"

Kevin Schafer/Alamy

Notice how the roots of the mangrove tree are interconnected, just like the ideas in students' books.

TEACHING

Draw students' attention to a small part of the text, one they might skip by. Then, ask students to turn and talk about parts of the book that could connect to that small part.

"I realized that when I was reading about toys and fast food at home, I sometimes did what you guys did. I thought about this or that person or idea almost as if I had blinders on, and just thought about what the text said in a particular place. I'm going to go back to one of those places that seemed trivial to me when I read the text last night, and this time I'm going to try to see if maybe this idea is rooted into a whole intertwined system that spans the whole text. Watch me do that." I displayed the excerpt as I read it aloud.

> *Every month about 90 percent of American children between the ages of three and nine visit a McDonald's. The seesaws, slides, and pits full of plastic balls have proven to be an effective lure. "But when it gets down to brass tacks," a* Brandweek *article on fast food notes, "the key to attracting kids is toys, toys, toys." . . . "A successful promotion easily doubles or triples the weekly sales volume of children's meals. The chains often distribute numerous versions of a toy, encouraging repeat visits by small children and adult collectors who hope to obtain complete sets . . . ."*

"I could just brush this part aside, but instead, I'll look for its roots. I'll ask, 'How might this part fit with what happened before?' I'll think go back over what we I've already read, and name parts that *might* fit.

As often as you can, fold in references to your out-of-school reading life: You are a mentor reader to your students, and the anecdotes you share provide a model of what an adult reading life can look like.

"Well, let me think. Were toys mentioned before? No, this is the first time Eric Schlosser wrote about toys. I guess this part also talks about kids. Were kids mentioned before? Not really, right, because this is all about fast food. Oh wait, I remember kids coming up right near the beginning of the book when Eric Schlosser wrote about how the McDonald brothers closed their first burger restaurant and put in the Speedee Service System. He talked about how they wanted more families to come into the restaurant, and families have lots of kids."

I flipped back to that part on pages 19 and 20. "Okay, how might this new part fit with what happened before?" I skimmed through the passage, tracing my finger down the page.

"Hmm, . . . Could this connect to the part where it says that the McDonald brothers were 'tired of their teenage customers?' Remember how they wanted to get rid of their teenage customers and attract families instead? I'm thinking that maybe the toys and the playgrounds are another way to attract families, because the book mentions small children and adults get the toys, but it never mentions teenagers. This part has roots earlier in the book."

Debrief, naming the transferable work you modeled.

"Did you see how I started by identifying something that felt insignificant, and then I pushed myself to study it, aware it might link to the central ideas in text? I identified other parts that *might* fit, and I studied those parts thinking, 'How might this part fit with what came before?'"

ACTIVE ENGAGEMENT

Rally students to try this work with you. Distribute another part of the book for clubs to study, and set them up to try the strategy.

"There are a couple of hard things here. One is to find parts that sort of, somehow, go together. The other is to think about *how* they go together, to ask questions and mark comparisons and hunches that bridge the two. Usually an idea, event, or person is connected to *many* parts of the book, just like that complicated mangrove root system. I'm going to distribute a passage that I think sort of goes with what we just read," and I gestured to the section about toys luring kids back to McDonald's. "We read this section about soda a couple of days ago when we were first beginning to figure out the central idea. But now that we've zeroed in on that part about toys and fast food, does that change how we see the section about soda? Will you and your book club study this new part, thinking, 'How might the part that we just read together fit with this part that came before?'" I distributed copies to students and asked them to start studying.

The nation's three major beverage manufacturers are now spending large sums to increase the amount of soda that American children consume. Coca-Cola, Pepsi, and Cadbury-Schweppes (the maker of Dr Pepper) control 90.3 percent of the U.S. market, but have been hurt by declining sales in Asia. Americans already drink soda at an annual rate of about fifty-six gallons per person—that's nearly six hundred twelve-ounce cans of soda per person. Coca-Cola has set itself the goal of raising consumption of its products in the United States by at least 25 percent a year. The adult market is stagnant; selling more soda to kids has become one of the easiest ways to meet sales projections. "Influencing elementary school students is very important to soft drink marketers," an article in the January 1999 issue of Beverage Industry explained, "because children are still establishing their tastes and habits." Eight-year-olds are considered ideal customers; they have about sixty-five years of purchasing in front of them. "Entering the schools makes perfect sense," the trade journal concluded.

The fast food chains also benefit enormously when children drink more soda. The chicken nuggets, hamburgers, and other main courses sold at fast food restaurants usually have the lowest profit margins. Soda has by far the highest. "We at McDonald's are thankful," a top executive once told the New York Times, "that people like drinks with their sandwiches." Today McDonald's sells more Coca-Cola than anyone else in the world. The fast food chains purchase Coca-Cola syrup for about $4.25 a gallon. A medium Coke that sells for $1.29 contains roughly 9 cents of syrup. Buying a large Coke for $1.49 instead, as the cute girl behind the counter always suggests, will add another 3 cents' worth of syrup— and another 17 cents in pure profit for McDonald's.

Move from club to club, sharing tips to lift the level of student work.

As I moved among the clubs, I coached, saying things such as:

- "What idea was the author getting across in *this* excerpt?"

- "Is there a central idea developing from *that* excerpt to *this* excerpt?"

- "Pay attention to the author's word choice. What specifically is the author saying about this idea?"

- "How does this idea develop? Does the author introduce it? Confirm it? Challenge it? Revise it?"

LINK

Add the new work to the anchor chart. Encourage clubs to choose a part of their reading to track to focus their work.

"Especially in longer nonfiction texts, authors will include ideas, events, and people that initially seem insignificant. Instead of brushing these parts off, it pays off to think, 'How might this part fit with what came before?'" I added this point to our anchor chart.

If this excerpt will be challenging for some students to read, you might gather those students close and say, "Listen as I read a bit, and keep thinking about how this part connects to what we read earlier." Then, you could read aloud the excerpt to students so that they are freed up to practice the skill work.

To Make the Most of Your
Nonfiction Chapter Books . . .

- Orient yourself to the text.
    - Review the front cover and table of contents.
    - Read the front matter to spark questions and ideas.
- Notice fascinating parts and mull them over to prepare for rich conversations.
- Determine possible central ideas.
    - Use pop-out sentences and headings.
    - Locate details across sections and think, "How do these details fit together?"
- Rethink central ideas in light of new evidence.
- Consider how embedded stories connect to central ideas.
- **Study how ideas, events, or people are developed across the text.**
    - **Ask, "How might this part fit with what came before?"**

"In addition to the other reading work you'll do today, will you and your club consider how parts of your book that might seem less significant could fit together to lead to central ideas? You might even look back and flag parts where that idea showed up earlier in the text. Be ready to bring those ideas to your club conversation. Off you go to get started!"

Supporting Students as They Analyze the Role Parts of the Text Play

BY NOW, most students will be nearing the end of their first book-club book, and it's possible some book clubs are onto their second book. Look for students to be approximating a repertoire of work as they read today. That is, students starting a new book are probably previewing the text and reading the front matter, whereas students nearing the end of the book are more apt to be revising their understanding of the text's central ideas in light of their new reading and their book-club conversations.

One line of work that tends to be fairly challenging for students is analyzing the role that parts of the text play in relation to the whole text. When students can do this work well, they can better understand how ideas, events, and people in a text are developed. This work also helps students learn to read like writers. As they pay attention to the role played by each part of another writer's piece, they become increasingly likely to pay attention to the role played by each part of their own writing.

However, students tend to talk about parts of the text in isolation, rather than considering their impact on the text as a whole. You taught into this work during your minilesson today, but you'll probably have students who could benefit from extra support.

Using Questions and Shared Experiences to Scaffold Students' Work

If students are not thinking about why parts of a text are included, you might provide them with a few questions that will push them to consider the role those parts play in relation to the whole text. The short list of questions you provide might include:

* "Why might the author have included this part?"
* "Does this part repeat something I learned earlier or is it new?"
* "What does this suggest about the whole topic?"

To provide an additional scaffold, you might first recruit students to practice with you on the text excerpt from *Fast Food Nation* that you used during today's active engagement, pages 53–54. You might say, "Let's try this together on that section you read earlier about the beverage manufacturers trying to sell soda to kids. You know the part well, so we'll start by asking ourselves these questions. Hmm, . . . Why might the author have included this part?"

Give students a bit of time to brainstorm in partnerships, and then share out a proficient response. You might say, "I'm thinking that one reason the author included this part is to give more evidence for one of the central ideas, that fast food companies take advantage of people to make money. It seems like this *part* is an example of how fast food companies take advantage of people—by trying to get kids hooked on soda!" You'll want to deliberately incorporate some academic language as you model, saying things like, *this part gives more evidence for the central idea*, *introduces a new perspective*, *proposes a solution to the problem*, *explains the effect of a cause*, *answers a question posed earlier*, and so on. You might even chart phrases like these for students.

You could quickly try out all three questions on the shared text, alternating between posing a question, channeling students to turn and talk in partnerships, and sharing out proficient responses. After a few minutes of trying the work together, students could dive into their own books, identify parts that might be important, and talk to determine how those parts could fit with the whole text.

Be sure to send students off with their own copy of these questions so they can reference them as they read independently and as they talk in their book clubs. You can print these questions from the online resources.

Rereading the Whole Text to Let New Thinking Emerge

Research shows that when a reader rereads a text he or she can read with high levels of accuracy, fluency, and comprehension, a reader's comprehension increases by up to 75% on a second read. This is significant. While you wouldn't want to suggest that, to boost their comprehension, students reread an entire chapter book immediately after reading it for the first time, we have found great success in teaching kids that they can read a passage once to get the gist, and then again to get a deeper understanding.

You might pull a small group today to support this kind of rereading work. Once students have gathered with their books and reader's notebooks, you could launch into a quick teach. "Readers, sometimes the first time you read through a text, when you're reading to figure out what the heck is going on, you miss things that end up being super-important later. It can help to think of your first read as a read to help you get the gist. The read goes quicker, and you push through, trying to get the big parts. Once you've got the gist of what's going on, you can think about parts that might be important and then go back and reread those parts. Rereading those parts with the gist of the text in mind can help you identify things that *now*, in the light of the whole text (or the whole text you've read so far), emerge as important."

Then, you'll want to set students up with a lot to do. "Will you try this right now? Think over what you've read recently and identify some parts that might be worth reading. These could be parts that seemed kind of important or parts that were a little confusing that you want to come back to. Then, reread those parts with your minds on high, on the lookout for things that now, in the light of the whole text, seem important."

Instead of jumping right in to coach one student, sit back for a minute and give kids time to get started. You might use gestures or lean prompts to launch all kids into the work. Once all students are working, you can move around the circle, coaching in with quick tips as students work. You might say, "Pay attention to details—details you didn't notice before might emerge as important now that you've got the gist of the text." "Ask yourself how the part you just reread might fit with the whole text."

FIG. 6–1   Caitlin uses sketches to trace how an idea is developed across the early chapters in her book.

FIG. 6–2   Wing Cam maps out how a central idea in her text evolved, leading her to a clearer sense of the author's central idea.

Analyzing Writing about Reading in Clubs

To launch their club conversations, channel students to select a piece of writing about reading they are proud of and to share it in their clubs. Set them up to give feedback in a few specific areas.

"Readers, will you open up your reading notebook or your book to a page where you did some writing about reading you're proud of?" I gave students about thirty seconds to find a spot. "To kick off your club conversation today, will you take a few minutes to study the writing about reading your clubmates have been doing and give them some feedback? Be ready to give them feedback about whether they've kept their writing about reading brief, whether they're tracking central ideas, and whether they're revising their thinking over time.

"Decide if you'd rather study one notebook all together and give feedback or rotate notebooks or books and jot feedback on Post-it notes. Once you've got a decision made, start reading and giving feedback."

I gave students about ten minutes to work, while I rotated from club to club, offering quick tips to support their writing about reading and talk.

SESSION 6 HOMEWORK

READING TO TRACE THE DEVELOPMENT OF IDEAS, EVENTS, OR INDIVIDUALS ACROSS YOUR TEXT

Tonight, in addition to reading forward in your text for at least thirty to forty minutes, will you also spend some time rereading? Continue to trace how one of the ideas, events, or individuals you started tracking in school is developed across your text. Don't just flag parts where the idea, event, or individual is mentioned. Instead, study them to see if you can name *how* the idea, event, or individual is being developed. Jot enough notes about this that you'll be prepared to teach your partner about how one idea, event, or individual is developed tomorrow. You can use one of the note-taking strategies you saw in your club, or you can develop your own.

Self-Assessing and Goal-Setting

IN THIS SESSION

TODAY YOU'LL teach students that readers use tools such as anchor charts to reflect on their growth and set goals.

TODAY YOUR STUDENTS will draw upon their self-assessment and goal-setting to push themselves to higher-level reading work.

MINILESSON

CONNECTION

Share a story about a goal you worked toward and how you took stock of your progress toward that goal. Link this story to the work readers have done with their nonfiction chapter books.

"I'm not sure you know this, but there was a time in my life when I thought of myself as a runner. I even timed myself to see how fast I ran when I ran a mile. The funny thing was, even though I ran several times a week, I found that I wasn't getting any better. My time stayed the same. So then I decided to study my running closely to see what I was doing well and where I needed some work. I realized that I was moving pretty quickly on flat surfaces and that it was running up steep hills that was really killing my time. I developed a plan to tackle that: adding more hills into my runs.

"I'm sharing this with you because this is similar to the work you've been doing as readers. When you started reading your longer, nonfiction chapter books a week ago, I challenged you to learn how to read these longer nonfiction books as well as you could. You've been working to accomplish that goal, but your work is not over."

Name the teaching point.

"Today I want to remind you that whenever you want to outgrow yourself, it helps to pause and take stock. One way readers do this is they look over all they've learned and ask, 'Am I doing these things when the book calls for them?' Then, they set goals to further lift the level of their work."

TEACHING

Explain how readers use tools, such as an anchor chart, to self-assess.

"One tool that's particularly helpful when you're pausing to take stock of your reading is the anchor chart, which captures the big things you've learned about in this bend." I gestured toward the "To Make the Most of Your Nonfiction Chapter Books . . ." chart and then continued.

"You can turn the anchor chart into a checklist, adding boxes next to each part of the checklist. Then, you can read each part of the checklist and ask, 'Am I doing these things when the book calls for them?' If you are doing that thing consistently, you'll be able to point to parts of the text or parts of your writing about reading where you did that work. If you notice you're not doing something at all, or if you're not doing it when the book calls for it, that thing can become a goal you to work toward." I added boxes to the anchor chart as I talked.

> **ANCHOR CHART**
>
> To Make the Most of Your
> Nonfiction Chapter Books . . .
>
> ☐ Orient yourself to the text.
> ☐ Review the front cover and table of contents.
> ☐ Read the front matter to spark questions and ideas.
> ☐ Notice fascinating parts and mull them over to prepare for rich conversations.
> ☐ Determine possible central ideas.
> ☐ Use pop-out sentences and headings.
> ☐ Locate details across sections and think, "How do these details fit together?"
> ☐ Rethink central ideas in light of new evidence.
> ☐ Consider how embedded stories connect to central ideas.
> ☐ Study how ideas, events, or people are developed across the text.
> ☐ Ask, "How might this part fit with what came before?"

Across your teaching today, you'll communicate a few main points to students. You'll teach them that they can use tools to self-assess their progress, and that it's important to find multiple pieces of evidence showing how you worked toward a goal, not just one example. You'll also emphasize that noticing things that you're not doing well is fantastic, because it means you have something to work toward. You might play up these messages if they are newer to your students.

Choose a part of the checklist you know is trickier for students. Demonstrate for students how you self-assess your work and set goals with that part of the checklist.

"Let me show you what I mean. I'll start with the bullet that says 'Revise the central ideas in light of new evidence.' I have to ask myself, 'Am I doing this work when the book calls for it?'" I modeled flipping through some of the writing about reading in my notebook and some of my annotations in the book.

Lingering on one page in my notebook, I said, "Oh, I've definitely been doing a *little* work revising my thinking about the central idea in light of new evidence. Remember how we went from thinking that fast food companies were taking advantage of workers to thinking fast food companies were taking advantage of everyone, including kids and workers? That was one time I revised my thinking. But, I'm not sure I see any other evidence that I've revised my thinking, and this is work I should be doing pretty regularly as I read."

"So, a new goal I need to work on is revising my thinking about the central ideas more often. I want to push myself to try that once a day. I'll jot that goal down, and then I can start working on it as I read today."

ACTIVE ENGAGEMENT

Pass out copies of the anchor chart made into a checklist. Ask partners to select one part of the checklist to study and ask, "Am I doing this work when the book calls for it?"

"Are you ready to try this? With your partner, choose a part of the checklist you'd both like to study first. Once you've got a part in mind, spend a minute or two on your own revisiting your book and your writing about reading. As you do, ask yourself, 'Am I doing this work when the book calls for it?' Prepare to share what you find, along with your evidence, with your partner."

I gave students about two minutes to study their own writing about reading and then said, "Share in your partnerships. Remember to push for evidence and consistency saying, 'Can you show me where you did that?' or 'Did you do that across your book?'"

LINK

Restate the teaching point, and send students off with a lot of work to do.

"Whenever you want to get better at something, remember it pays to pause and take stock. As a reader, you want to especially ask yourself, 'Am I doing all the things I could be doing when the book calls for it?' Then, you can set goals to make your work even better than it already is.

"As you head off today, spend just a few minutes self-assessing your work, not the whole reading period. Then pick up your books and continue reading with your goals in mind, making a conscious effort to further lift the level of your work by working toward your goals."

You send a powerful message to your students when you keep your own reader's notebook where you try the work alongside them.

Study how ideas, events or people are developed.

Plan to work towards that goal:
- Take notes in order of events (chronological order)
- Take notes as a story/event/idea/people goes along and track that as it builds and develops
- Use different perspectives to show how the beliefs of other vary and how that can develop our ideas
- You can track dates and how things may change or develop from date to date
- How ideas can change over time, for example Christopher Columbus's intentions might be different to what they appear to be towards historians.

FIG. 7–1 Will jots a plan showing ways he'll work toward his goal.

Supporting Goal-Setting and the Work of the Bend

WHILE STUDENTS ARE SELF-ASSESSING AND GOAL-SETTING, you'll want to support their work. You might move from table to table, doing brief check-ins to lift the level of students' work. The table below outlines several predictable problems you might see as students self-assess, along with ways you can quickly teach in to offer support.

You could also use this time to pull small groups to support the teaching work you did this bend. If you notice that four students all set a goal to work toward one area of the checklist with more consistency, such as developing initial ideas about what the text is teaching, you could gather those students together. Resist the urge to reteach your earlier minilesson. What will benefit students most is time to practice while you coach in, so you'll want to give a quick reminder of your earlier teaching, talking for less than a minute, and then launch students into trying the work in their books while you coach in briefly, moving from student to student.

If you notice . . .	Then you can teach . . .
Students simply check off the boxes on the checklist.	"Readers look for evidence of ways they've worked toward their goals in their books and writing about reading. They're careful not to check off part of the checklist as complete unless they can point to specific evidence of where they did that work. Try that out right now. Go back into your work and find evidence of where you did different kinds of work."
Students seem discouraged when they identify things they have not yet done or are not yet doing regularly.	"It's so exciting that you're finding goals you can work toward. When you can identify something you can do even better as a reader, a next step, then you have a clear sense of how you can make your work even better. Congratulations!"
Students consider it sufficient to try something only once.	"People who work toward goals typically have to practice multiple times before their skills improve. Will you ask yourself, 'Am I doing these things whenever the book calls for it?' You might only read the prelude once, but you'll need to read on the lookout for central ideas across the entire book."
Students set a goal, then put the goal aside and continue reading.	"Readers generate plans for how they'll work toward their goals. They think, 'What can I do first, second, third to meet this goal?' Then, they put their plan into action. Let's try this. Name your goal, and then let's generate and chart ways you can work toward that goal."

"Speed Dating" Research Topics

Introduce the focus of Bend II. Channel students to preview collections of resources to choose a topic for further study.

"You're becoming pros at reading longer nonfiction chapter books, and that's one kind of reading that nonfiction readers do. Another kind of reading nonfiction readers do is take a topic and then read a bunch of texts on that topic, building up their knowledge on that topic as they go. That's the kind of nonfiction reading we'll start tomorrow, in the next bend of our unit.

"I started gathering texts on a whole host of topics I think will really interest you: atomic bombs, the *Titanic*, teen activism, climate change, genetic engineering, diseases and illnesses, and outer space exploration. I don't just want to assign you to a topic. Instead, I want you to get a chance to try out these topics so you can figure out which ones you really want to spend a week or so studying.

"I put a few articles and trade books on each topic in stations around the room that are labeled with big signs. You probably won't have time to visit *all* the stations in the room, so you'll want to start with the stations you think you're most interested in. Scan the articles, study the trade books, and ask yourself, 'Is this a topic I want to study further?' Then, move to the next station. You'll probably want to keep a list of topics you're interested in studying in order of priority."

You'll find text sets on a host of topics in the online resources. You can, of course, substitute in topics that are more relevant to your students or that align with your current content area focus. Pay particular attention to the text sets that include lower-level texts, so you can steer students toward those topics, as needed.

SESSION 7 HOMEWORK

WORKING TOWARD GOALS AND TOPIC SELECTION

Tonight, split your reading time in half. For the first twenty minutes or so, continue reading on in your nonfiction chapter books. Work on the goals you set today as you read. Be sure to show evidence of how you worked toward your goals: flagged pages with quick jots, longer jots in your reading notebook, and so on.

For the second half of your reading time, will you keep studying the list of Bend II research projects to determine which will be most fascinating to study? I'm sending you home with a short snippet about each topic. Read over these, do a bit of research online if you can, and come into school tomorrow ready to let me know your decision.

Investigating Topics with Research Groups, and Synthesizing across Texts on That Topic

A Letter to Teachers

Dear Teachers,

This bend is all about teaching your students how to read to learn. In this bend, you equip students with the tried-and-true skills they need to approach a topic they're fascinated by, even if it's a topic they know very little about, and to learn all they can about that topic through their reading. Students will leave this bend with a toolkit of strategies that help them build background knowledge, synthesize what they learn across texts, and make strategic decisions about when they need to do a bit of on-the-run research to shore up their understanding of a text.

Reading to learn well will have a tremendous impact on your students' lives. Imagine one student is given a model rocket kit by her grandparents and doesn't have the slightest idea how to build a rocket that really works. Imagine a second student who realizes he doesn't have the faintest clue what the Donner Party is, and he's about to study it in history class. Or, picture a third student, scrolling through a friend's Facebook wall, when she comes across an unfamiliar reference. Instead of feeling discouraged or accepting confusion, your students will approach those new topics ready to learn all they can, equipped with the toolkit of strategies you provision them with in this bend.

As Bend II launches, you'll invite students to work in research groups, with each group researching a topic chosen from a list of fascinating options. You'll provide groups with a starter set of articles, trade books, and multimedia texts related to their topics. As students read across their text sets to learn as much as they can about their topics, you'll teach them how to problem solve independently, so that when they face points of trouble in the future, they can get themselves through those tricky points.

One way you'll support this is by teaching students to build up bits of background knowledge. In "You Can't Learn Much from Texts You Can't Read" (*Educational Leadership*, November 2002), Richard Allington suggests that reading multiple texts on a topic helps kids raise the level of their nonfiction reading. You'll teach students to begin with the most accessible texts on a topic before moving to more complex texts, which prepares students to read the more complex texts because they'll have accumulated some knowledge on the key vocabulary and concepts of the topic. You'll also teach students that when they encounter difficulty as they read, they can get support by turning to an easier text or an explanatory text, or they can do some targeted rereading. In this way, your teaching provisions students with a toolkit of strategies they can draw on whenever a class, text, or even conversation gets tough. You'll also teach students how to bring points of difficulty to their club for support, so that they can troubleshoot together when meaning breaks down.

Of course, this bend also supports students in lifting the level of their nonfiction reading skills. As the bend launches, you'll support transference from Bend I by bringing back the "To Make the Most of Your Nonfiction Chapter Book . . ." anchor chart and teaching students that everything they learned how to do in one type of nonfiction text, they can do in other nonfiction texts. Then, you'll build off this work by teaching students how to summarize, so they can construct short versions of the critical points in a text to hold on to what each text is teaching. Since students are reading multiple texts within a text set, supporting cross-text synthesis work will be critical. As they read across texts on a topic, you'll teach students to consider how their new learning fits with, contradicts, or extends their previous learning and to integrate the new information they are learning into their existing notes. Later, you'll extend this work, helping students grow their own ideas off of the information they've learned.

As texts get more complex, students' knowledge of the keywords of their topic becomes intricately linked to their knowledge of the central ideas and concepts of their topic. To help students better understand the central ideas and concepts related to their topic, you'll teach students to sort and re-sort the vocabulary words they are learning. They might sort the vocabulary they are learning once by central idea, and then again based on whether the words are positive or negative, and then a third time to show how the words relate to one another.

During the share in Session 7, you invited students to identify topics they were interested in studying in Bend II. Before you launch students into their new research groups, you'll want to take some time to arrange students into research groups. There are a few ways you could do this. If the majority of your students are reading at or above grade level, you could group students together by interest and by ability to work productively together. If you have many students reading below grade level, you might decide to group students roughly by reading level, so you can supply kids with a collection of texts that are at or near to their reading levels.

Once students are grouped together, you'll want to provision each club of four students with a collection of texts on a topic they expressed interest in studying during the share in Session 7. If you skipped this share, we recommend you pause the unit for a day to give students time to "speed date" several topics and identify the topics they are most interested in. We've suggested several topics that tend to fascinate middle-schoolers, but you will want to personalize topics based on your students' interests. In the online resources for this unit, we've included suggestions for text sets on atomic bombs, the *Titanic*, teen activism, climate change, genetic engineering, diseases and illnesses, and outer space exploration. Each text set we've recommended includes texts on a range of reading levels. We've marked the text sets that include significantly lower-level texts, and you might choose to channel students reading below grade level to those topics. If you are a content-area teacher, you can of course substitute text sets on other topics. If you make this change, study the text sets in the online resources closely and create similar text sets for your students. Whatever topics you select, make sure you provision students with enough texts to keep them reading for a week-and-a-half.

We deliberately constructed each text set so it includes trade books, articles, and video texts. If possible, students will benefit from having access to computers, tablets, or smart phones so they can do some quick, on-the-run research. You'll want to do whatever you can to get copies of the trade books for students. The trade books are engaging for kids, and they ensure kids read through a volume of text on their topics. Note that some of the trade books are significantly easier than others. Even if your students are mostly reading at or above grade level, we still recommend that you get some of these significantly easier texts for your text sets. As mentioned earlier, reading easier texts helps students build up a bit of background knowledge on a topic. You'd be amazed at how much can be learned from a book on Mars written at a second-grade reading level.

The way you distribute texts to students will communicate your expectations for volume. If you only distribute one text to students at a time, kids will most likely only read that one text. Instead, you'll want to provision students with a bin of texts and several trade books so they can read across multiple texts in a single reading period. You'll also want to use language that keeps kids cycling through texts, saying things like, "Which *texts* will you read today?" and "Which text will you read *next*?"

You won't want to miss out on the fun, so you'll want to choose a topic for the class to study during your read-aloud and minilessons. Across Bend II, we recommend that you study GMOs. In the online resources, we've assembled a collection of articles and videos on this topic and also suggested trade books you could order. You might invite a group of kids who need more support to study this same topic, as your whole-class modeling with the topic will give those kids a leg up on their research.

You'll see that the homework across this bend channels students to continue reading texts on their topic. If you don't have a large enough volume of texts for all your middle schoolers to take home sufficient reading material, you might need to modify this. You could ask students to continue reading nonfiction chapter books, to read any high-interest nonfiction that interests them, or to take on some courses of study in fiction, perhaps reading several books in a genre or by an author. Above all, it matters that students maintain their volume of reading and continue to move through about forty pages of text a day.

To creating a culture of resiliency and problem solving!
Katie

Read-Aloud

*Building Up a Bit of Background Knowledge
When You Encounter a New Topic*

GETTING READY

✓ Group students based on the topic they would like to study in this bend and/or their reading levels. Have students gather in the meeting area with their new research groups.

✓ Set students up with a partner in their research group to talk with during whole-class lessons in this bend.

✓ Choose topics for each research club, as well as a class topic, and prepare starter sets of materials for each, including nonfiction trade books, articles, videos, and other digital resources. In the online resources you'll find text sets for the following topics: atomic bombs, the *Titanic*, teen activism, climate change, genetic engineering, diseases and illnesses, and outer space exploration. Add chart paper to each bin.

✓ Select a text from your class text set to demonstrate how to preview to determine common subtopics. We used "The Battle Over GMOs" (see Conducting the Read-Aloud).

✓ Create a list of subtopics for your class topic on chart paper (see Conducting the Read-Aloud).

✓ Prepare to read aloud the easiest text in your class text set. We chose "So what is genetic engineering?" A link to this text is available in the online resources (see Conducting the Read-Aloud).

✓ Begin the "To Research a New Topic . . ." anchor chart (see Link).

IN THIS SESSION

TODAY YOU'LL remind students that when readers begin researching a new topic, they draw on tried-and-true strategies to begin learning about a topic.

TODAY YOUR STUDENTS will preview to get the gist of their topic, pore over easier resources to build a bit of background knowledge, and write or teach others to solidify their learning.

CONNECTION

Remind students of the major work of this bend. Explain that this bend will equip them to more confidently tackle tricky topics they encounter in all their classes moving forward.

I invited students to gather in the meeting area and sit with their new research groups. I asked them to choose a partner in their group to talk with during lessons. Once they had gathered I said, "Readers, today's an exciting day. In the last bend, you read a ton of writing by a single author. That's one thing readers of nonfiction do. And yesterday, I mentioned that another thing readers of nonfiction do is take a topic and create text sets on that topic, compiling a bunch of different short texts. Then, they read lightly and quickly on that topic, thinking across the texts, so they begin to grow knowledge about that topic.

"This work will help you learn more about the topics you chose to study, but it also matters tremendously to your lives today. You don't want to be the kinds of kids who wait in the dark for a teacher to teach you everything. Definitely not! There would be so many things you'd never learn because you'd just be sitting back, waiting for someone else to teach you. Instead, you want to be the kid who reads to learn all you can.

"Luckily, building up background knowledge on a topic is not magic. It's not a thing that some people have and some people don't. Background knowledge is something you can get yourself, if you're willing to put in a little bit of work."

CONDUCTING THE READ-ALOUD

Invite students to help you research a whole-class topic. Demonstrate how you preview a text to determine common subtopics.

"I chose a research project for us to study as a class during our lessons, one I hope will fascinate all of you since it affects your day-to-day lives: genetically modified foods, also known as GMOs. For our read-aloud time today, I thought we could start studying this topic, doing the things that you'll recall researchers do whenever they study a new and fairly unfamiliar topic. Will you help me?"

I set the bin of texts in front of me, and said, "Let's do what readers do when they begin researching a new topic. I'll bet most of you remember from earlier grades that readers often survey all the resources they have, looking from one text to the next to see which subtopics show up repeatedly. Identifying common subtopics helps them focus their research."

I pulled out a few texts, grabbed one titled "The Battle Over GMOs," and said, "Hmm, . . . help me look across the title, subheadings, and the images to see what subtopics are coming up. It's titled 'The Battle Over GMOs' and then there are some subheadings: 'Are GMOs the answer to feeding a hungry world, or Frankenfoods that put the environment—and us—at risk?,' 'I Don't Think We Know Enough,' and 'A Boon to Farmers?' And check out these images." I briefly displayed the two images from the article.

"Turn and tell your partner what subtopics are already emerging from this text." As students talked, I quickly jotted a list.

Genetically Modified Foods Subtopics

- Kinds of GMOs
- Disagreements around GMOs

Recruit students to look across multiple texts on a topic and identify repeating subtopics. Chart the subtopics they discover.

"To really get a sense of the subtopics that matter for this topic, we have to look across many texts to see which subtopics repeat. I'm going to distribute some other texts to your group. Look across them to see what subtopics we should add to our list." I quickly passed two or three texts out to each group.

This is your chance to sell kids on the topic the entire class will research during minilessons, so you'll really want to play this part up and get your class excited about the topic.

As students talked, I voiced over. "Let me give you a tip: some of your texts won't have headings for each part or tables of contents. In those situations, look at the text features and scan the article for repeating words and concepts."

After a minute and a half, I gathered students together. "You found several subtopics that seem to be emerging across these texts. I'll add them to our list, and we'll keep these subtopics in mind as we start reading."

Genetically Modified Organisms Subtopics

- Kinds of GMOs
- Disagreements around GMOs
- What GMOs are
- How genetic engineering works

Next, explain that readers read super-easy texts to build up their background knowledge on a topic. Coach them as they sequence texts from easiest to hardest to determine which text to read first.

"We have one more thing to do before we're ready to start reading. Whenever you're researching a new topic, it helps to start with simple texts, the kind that you would find in the little kids' section of the bookstore, because they equip you with the background knowledge you need to read harder texts later. Easier texts are sometimes (but not always!) shorter, and they often give an overview of the topic.

"Hmm, . . . let's see which texts are easiest. I don't think we should start with 'Genetically Engineered Salmon Approved for Consumption,' because that feels too narrow. Our goal is to get an overview of the whole topic. Plus, that article looks pretty complicated. Look at the texts you're holding. Do they seem like easier texts we should read first, or harder texts we should read after we've got a bit of background knowledge? Sequence them with your group."

I gave students about a minute to talk, and then called them back. "It sounds like the article 'So what is genetic engineering?' will give us the best overview of the topic before we dive into the specifics. That makes a lot of sense to me. Let's start with that one."

Read aloud, setting up students to listen with their minds on high. Pause to demonstrate how you grow your thinking and to channel students to share what they are learning with a partner.

"Here's the thing. You'll probably also recall that when nonfiction readers want to quickly build up a bit of background knowledge, they have to read simpler texts shamelessly and intensely, with their minds on high, trying to learn all they can from them. Ready to try it?"

I displayed "So what is genetic engineering?" and started reading aloud.

Your students will learn so much about their topics if they're willing to dive into the easiest texts first. You'll want to really play this point up so students willingly take on this essential work.

So what is genetic engineering?

'Engineering' is a fancy word for building something. So genetic engineering (often just called GE) is building something with genes. Clever scientists have learned to spot which gene does what in making a new organism.

"So, it seems like this part is giving us a definition of what genetic engineering is, and it's got something to do with how scientists build things out of your genes, which it sounds like you may know from science class are things that help make up a creature. They're the tiny parts that determine what an organism's traits will be. I'll continue reading. Keep your mind on high, working to learn all you can from this text."

They've found out that simple organisms like bacteria or viruses often have genes which are useful because they can be snipped out and put—<u>spliced</u>—into plant genes. Doing this could give the plant special new abilities like resisting diseases.

"Are you already learning a ton? Whisper with a partner about what you're learning." I gave students thirty seconds to talk, and then continued.

"I heard some of you saying that genetic engineering means actually taking genes out of one organism and putting them into another. Wow, that is fascinating. A few of you questioned whether it would be a good idea to take genes from things like bacteria and viruses and put them into plants. I have the same question too! Let's keep going, collecting background knowledge, and seeing where the text heads next."

But this can be rather like grabbing a scorpion so it can't nip you with its claws. You know it's safe to handle since its claws can't reach you but—*ow!*—it's got a sting in its tail you didn't know about. There may be a 'sting in the tail' which comes from splicing strange genes into other organisms—from viruses to plants, for example. No one can be quite certain what will happen. It is <u>unpredictable</u>. Genes can do unexpected and unintended things and nobody can ever be quite sure what. So it is wise to be very careful.

"Readers, I'm sensing the text is shifting directions a bit. The earlier part we read talked about benefits of genetic engineering. This last part suggests there may be problems. Would you talk to each other about the new information we got here, and compare it to what we learned earlier about GMOs?"

I gave the students a minute to talk, and then I continued, "I heard some of you thinking about what we were wondering earlier—whether GMOs are always such a good idea. You talked about how this part of the text gives us some new information about GMOs—it's hard to predict what will happen when splicing genes from one organism to another."

Read on, then set students up to teach each other what they've learned so far about the topic to solidify their understanding.

"Let's continue reading and building our background knowledge. Stay alert to everything the text is teaching you about this topic. As you know, teaching others is a way to solidify what you know. After I read, you'll have a chance to teach your partner *everything* you learned in this part."

I read on:

> ## What can genetic engineering do?
>
> Genetically modified organisms, GMOs, (which are mostly plants) are mostly <u>transgenic</u>, which means they contain genes pinched from something else like bacteria, viruses, other plants or even animals. By snipping a gene which does something useful from one organism and splicing it into another, say a crop plant, scientists can get the plant to grow bigger or faster or make more for people to eat. Or the plant could be made to be more nutritious with more protein or minerals or vitamins. Some crop plants can be made to grow in salty water or very little water—good for very dry countries. Others could be engineered to <u>resist disease</u> which could protect kids against nasty illnesses like polio or measles.

"Go ahead, teach each other what you learned in this part."

Soon, I paused students to offer a tip. "Use the words that are important to the topic as you teach."

After a minute, I called students back. "This simple article about genetic engineering gave us a tiny bit of background knowledge about some big concepts and key vocabulary. Now that we understand a bit more, we can move to a slightly harder article, one like 'The Battle Over GMOs.'"

Debrief, pointing out some of the reading work students did to build their background knowledge.

"Readers, we've already gotten a better sense of this topic, just from reading a short part of one text. To grow background knowledge quickly, it's important to stay alert as you read, naming back to yourself what the text is teaching you, letting the text raise questions for you, and noticing times when the text shifts direction or moves into new terrain. It helps to read as if you are preparing to teach someone about the topic, whether or not you actually get to do the teaching."

Purpose matters. Look for places where you can emphasize the reasons why you ask your students to do particular work.

LINK

Link the work students did today during the read-aloud to the work they can do whenever they encounter a new topic. Introduce an anchor chart that captures the major work you taught.

"I charted some of the big moves we made to research our shared topic that you can try out whenever you're researching a new topic." I revealed a new anchor chart.

> **ANCHOR CHART**
>
> To Research a New Topic . . .
>
> - **Preview texts to identify repeating subtopics.**
> - **Build up a bit of background knowledge quickly.**
>   - **Sequence your texts. Start with easier texts—even videos!**
>   - **Teach others what you're learning.**

"I've provisioned you and your research group with a starter bin of articles and trade books on the topics you selected. You'll only have about fifteen minutes to read today. Will you use this time to preview your topic and start building up a tiny bit of background knowledge? I added some big pieces of chart paper to your bins so you can chart the subtopics you find. Off you go!"

INDEPENDENT READING

Quick Table Conferences to Support Students in Building Background Knowledge

Building up background knowledge is important work, and you'll want to support all of your students as they take this on. You probably won't have time to call students together for longer small groups today. Instead, we recommend you lead quick table conferences as groups work.

Here are some tips you might provide while students are working in groups:

- **Coach students as they identify subtopics in their texts:** "As you're identifying subtopics, don't add each new subtopic to the list willy-nilly. First see if the new subtopics you're identifying fit with the subtopics that are already on your list or if you need to revise a subtopic you already have. Then, if the subtopic is not represented on your list, you can add it."

- **Coach kids as they sequence texts from easiest to hardest:** "When you want to do something hard, like run a marathon, you don't start with a 26.2-mile run. You start with a shorter run, maybe a mile or two, and you gradually work your way up. You can do the same thing when you're building up background knowledge. You start with the easiest text, and then move up to one that's slightly harder, and then one that's a little bit harder than that. Will you try that right now? Lay out your resources, and take a minute to preview them. Then, work with your partner to sequence them from easiest to hardest, and get started studying the easiest one together."

- **Remind students of what they know about note-taking from Bend I:** "Readers, I have to stop you. It looks like you've forgotten everything you learned about note-taking from the last bend of the unit. Your notes look like lists of facts. Glancing down at them, it's almost impossible to tell what's important! Remember these tips: You want to jot notes on central ideas, not just facts; you want your jotting to be quick, so it doesn't take more than 10% of your time; you want to revise your jots if new information makes you rethink what you jotted earlier. Will you start incorporating these tips into your notes right now? I'm going to admire your work as you do."

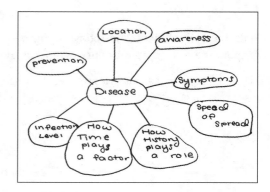

FIG. 8–1 A web of possible subtopics related to disease.

SHARE

Set groups up to generate a list of subtopics related to their topic. If time allows, encourage them to talk a bit about each subtopic once their list is generated.

"Readers, you've only been studying your topics for about fifteen minutes, but already, you're noticing a bunch of different subtopics. We've just got a few minutes left for reading today. Will you use this time to collaborate with your group to generate a list of the subtopics that tend to repeat across your texts? Once your list is generated, talk a bit about those subtopics. Did you learn anything about them as you read today? Do you know anything about those subtopics already? Share that knowledge with your group mates."

SESSION 8 HOMEWORK

BUILDING UP BACKGROUND KNOWLEDGE

Tonight, make a concerted effort to build up a bit of background knowledge on your topic. You can bring easy articles or books from the classroom home to read, search for "easy articles" or "kid articles" about your topic, or watch videos to get oriented. As you read texts and watch videos, jot notes about what you're learning. Make sure you capture the key vocabulary words and the central ideas the texts teach. Plan to spend at least thirty minutes building up your background knowledge tonight, so you're ready to hit the ground running with your research tomorrow. And, if you find any texts you think your whole group would benefit from studying, print them off or share them with your group electronically.

Drawing on All You Know to Tackle New Projects with More Skill

IN THIS SESSION

TODAY YOU'LL teach students that they can draw on all they know about reading nonfiction chapter books to help them read short texts in their nonfiction text sets with more skill and confidence.

TODAY YOUR STUDENTS will start reading their text sets with their research clubs, drawing on the strategies they learned for reading nonfiction chapter books as they begin digging into the shorter texts of their research text set.

GETTING READY

✔ Prepare to revise the title of the "To Make the Most of Your Nonfiction Chapter Books . . . " anchor chart (see Connection, Teaching and Active Engagement, and Homework).

✔ Display the article "The Battle Over GMOs" to demonstrate how students can draw on what they learned in Bend I to develop a sense of the central ideas of the article (see Teaching and Active Engagement).

✔ Provide a mini version of the "To Make the Most of Your Nonfiction Texts" anchor chart (see Homework).

MINILESSON

CONNECTION

Remind students of the work they did self-assessing at the end of Bend I. Channel partners to share what they learned to do well as nonfiction chapter book readers.

"Readers, will you pull out your copies of the 'To Make the Most of Your Nonfiction Chapter Books . . .' anchor chart? A few short days ago, you self-assessed your work to determine which of the things you'd learned how to do you were regularly doing and you set a goal to make your nonfiction chapter book reading even stronger. Will you take a minute to remind your partner about what you learned to do well as a nonfiction chapter book reader?"

A minute later, I said, "It would be such a shame to just disregard everything you learned just because you're no longer reading nonfiction chapter books!"

I revised the title of our "To Make the Most of Your Nonfiction Chapter Books . . ." chart to read "To Make the Most of Your Nonfiction Texts . . ."

ANCHOR CHART

To Make the Most of Your Nonfiction
~~Chapter Books~~ Texts . . .

- Orient yourself to the text.
  - Review the front cover and table of contents.
  - Read the front matter to spark questions and ideas.
- Notice fascinating parts and mull them over to prepare for rich conversations.
- Determine possible central ideas.
  - Use pop-out sentences and headings.
  - Locate details across sections and think, "How do these details fit together?"
- Rethink central ideas in light of new evidence.
- Consider how embedded stories connect to central ideas.
- Study how ideas, events, or people are developed across the text.
  - Ask, "How might this part fit with what came before?"

To Make the Most of Your Nonfiction Texts

 Name the teaching point.

"Today I want to teach you that when you start a new project, you aren't starting over totally from scratch. No way! Instead, you draw on all you know to tackle that new project. You can use all you've learned about reading nonfiction chapter books to help you more confidently read in your text sets."

TEACHING AND ACTIVE ENGAGEMENT

Recruit students to read a nonfiction article with you, using all they've learned about reading nonfiction chapter books to read a shorter article.

"Let's try this together. We'll read a new text, the one we identified as the second text we'd read in our text set—'The Battle Over GMOs.' As we read, let's use everything we learned how to do as nonfiction chapter book readers to help us read this brief nonfiction article well."

Demonstrate how you read a bullet on the chart and consider how that work could apply to a new kind of text. Rally students to preview the text with you, reading titles, subheadings, and captions.

I displayed the text, then glanced at our anchor chart. "Hmm, . . ." I touched the first bullet on the chart. "It says we have to read covers and front matter. Well, we definitely can't do that because there's no cover or introduction, right? Should we just skip that one? No way! How *could* that work for these texts?" I paused for a few seconds, leaving time for kids to think alongside me.

"I guess we could preview the article, since that's similar to previewing an entire book. To preview, we can look at the title, subheadings, and all the text features. I'll read them aloud. Be ready to share your thoughts and musings with a partner."

I read aloud the title, subheadings, and captions.

"This is fascinating, right? Share your thoughts and musings with your partner."

After a few moments, I shared some of what I heard students saying. "I heard some of you thinking about the subtitle, and noticing some of the images of genetically modified foods. A lot of you are thinking what I am—this article is going to take a tougher stance on GMOs. We'll likely learn more about the hazards of GMOs than we did in the last article."

Channel students to study the anchor chart and consider what work they'll need to do as readers at the beginning of the article. Then, read the first part of the article and practice that work.

"Okay, now that we've previewed, it's time to read. Look over the anchor chart and tell your partner what work you'll probably need to do at the beginning of the article."

Students shared that they'd probably need to notice thought-provoking points and develop some initial ideas about what the text is teaching. "Ready to try this work as I read on?"

The Battle Over GMOs

Are GMOs the answer to feeding a hungry world, or Frankenfoods that put the environment—and us—at risk?

By Alessandra Potenza / February 8, 2016

Thousands of people recently took to the streets in 400 cities worldwide. The cause of their anger? Not oppressive governments, unemployment, or income inequality, but apples that don't brown when sliced and corn that's bred to fight off insects. In short, GMOs—genetically modified organisms.

In Los Angeles, protesters chanted, "Hell no GMO!" In Strasbourg, France, demonstrators held a minute of silence in front of the European Parliament. And in Rio de Janeiro, Brazil, people accused GMO producers of "bioterrorism."

Your students will get more out of your demonstration if they are doing the thinking work alongside you. Posing questions and leaving brief pauses gives students the opportunity to try the work themselves, keeping them more intellectually engaged as you teach.

Your coaching cues students to consider what work the text is asking them to do. You want this work to become automatic for your students, so they do it whenever they read.

"Are you noticing any thought-provoking points? Getting an initial sense of what the text is teaching?" Students nodded, and I continued reading.

> GMOs are organisms whose DNA has been combined with a gene from an unrelated species to produce a desired trait. Some crops are genetically modified to survive herbicide sprays that kill weeds. Others are engineered to be more nutritious: A pink pineapple awaiting U.S. government approval has the same antioxidant that makes tomatoes red and may help prevent cancer. In November, the U.S. Food and Drug Administration approved the first genetically modified animal: a salmon engineered to grow to market size in about half the time as a regular salmon.
>
> But GMOs haven't been popular lately. Only 37 percent of Americans think they're safe to eat, according to the Pew Research Center. McDonald's recently refused to use a new genetically modified potato that produces less of a cancer-causing chemical when fried. Chipotle dropped GMOs from its U.S. offerings. And General Mills stopped using GMOs in original Cheerios after a yearlong campaign by environmentalists.

"Are your minds overflowing like mine? Share any thought-provoking points and your initial ideas about the central ideas in the text with your partner."

As students talked, I coached in, reminding them to apply strategies they'd learned earlier. To one partnership, I said, "Look back at the chart to see the kinds of thought-provoking points you might discuss, choose one, and try it."

To a partnership having trouble identifying a possible central idea, I said, "Remember to use our strategies to determine the central ideas. Look at the chart to remind yourself of those strategies if you're stuck."

Set students up to study the anchor chart again, noticing the work readers could do about one-third of the way into a text. Read on in the text, and then channel students to talk to share their thinking.

Then I said, "We're about one-third of the way through the article, and we've already got an initial sense of a central idea: that GMOs are not very popular. Decide with your partner what reading work you'll likely need to do as we read on."

Students suggested that in addition to thinking about thought-provoking ideas, they'd need to be ready to revise their thinking about the central ideas as they read on.

"Let's try it." I read aloud the next few paragraphs.

'I Don't Think We Know Enough'

> While some see GMOs as Frankenfoods that hurt the environment, and us, others see them as the most promising solution to feeding the world's population, which is expected to skyrocket from 7 billion today to 10 billion by 2050. The government agencies regulating GMOs in the U.S. say they're safe. But

some scientists and consumers argue that GMOs haven't been around long enough for us to know their long-term health effects.

"We're putting genes into crops that have never been in the food supply before," says Doug Gurian-Sherman, a scientist at the Center for Food Safety, a nonprofit organization opposing GMOs. "I don't think we know enough."

"How many of you got some new evidence that's leading you to revise your thinking about the central ideas?" Most students signaled that they had. "How many of you noticed thought-provoking lines, ones you could talk a lot about? Try talking about one of those things right now with a partner."

LINK

Restate the teaching point, and link the work students just did reading an article to the work they can do reading any nonfiction text. Set students up to make a reading plan and then to read.

"Do you see how the nonfiction reading work you learned to do while reading chapter books can help you learn to read *any* kind of nonfiction text well? Do you think if I showed you another text on your topic, maybe a longer article, you'd be able to do this same nonfiction reading work? What about if I showed you a video, a documentary? Once you learn how to do something well in one situation, you can use your skills to help you read other kinds of texts with even more skill and confidence.

"Before you head off to read, take just a minute to make a plan. What easier, overview texts will you start with today to help you build a little background knowledge? Are there particular subtopics you want to study as you read? Whatever you plan, make sure to read with your mind on high, and draw on all you know that readers of nonfiction texts do. Off you go!"

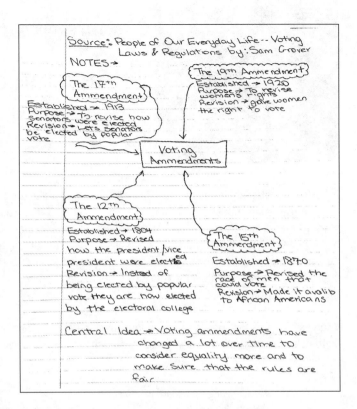

FIG. 9–1   The bends of this unit can easily be used in content-area classrooms. Here, Paige investigates voting rights in her social studies class and jots notes about the central ideas in her texts.

Teaching to Support Transference

GRANT WIGGINS in his article "What Is Transfer?" talks about how supporting transference should be a major goal of education. While comparing school to soccer, he argues that too much of school is clean, clear-cut drills, where skills are being practiced in isolation outside of a realistic context. Instead, he says that more time needs to be spent scrimmaging, learning to play what he calls the "'messy' game intelligently." Today, you'll want to get kids scrimmaging and then be ready to support them as they work.

Wiggins suggests that one way to support transference is by clearly naming the goal of transfer for students, so they realize that transferring what they know from one context to the next is expected. You named this goal clearly for students during your minilesson, but you'll want to look for additional opportunities to name transfer as a goal across varied contexts.

To transfer over what they know, students will need to consider how the skills and strategies they learned earlier apply in a new context with different kinds of texts. Some students might directly see how what they learned earlier transfers to a new context, while other students might need more tips. This table provides tips about how nonfiction reading work differs from chapter books to short texts and ways you can support students with transfer.

When reading nonfiction chapter books, students learned to . . .	When reading short texts in a research group, you can teach students . . .
Preview the cover and front matter, and develop thoughts and musings.	"Let me teach you how previewing is a bit different when reading short articles than nonfiction chapter books. Instead of reading the cover and the front matter to develop thoughts and musings, researchers often preview their articles to get a sense of the subtopics that repeat. "They can also preview individual articles, looking across the title, subheadings, and text features to determine what a specific article might teach and to develop some thoughts and musings as they preview."
Develop initial ideas about what the text is teaching and then revise the central ideas in light of new information.	"When you only read a two- or three-page article, the central ideas come at you quickly, and you don't have a lot of time to revise your understanding of the central ideas based on what you're learning. "Instead of revising your thinking about the central ideas as you read through *a single* text, when you're researching a topic across many texts, you have to revise your thinking about the central ideas as you read across all the texts on a topic. You get an initial sense of the central ideas, and then you read across multiple texts with those central ideas in mind."
Consider how small ideas, events, or people are developed over time.	"In the short articles you're reading now, there's not a lot of time for small ideas, events, or people to be developed over time because as soon as you meet someone new or learn about a new event, it's over! "Instead, you need to trace how ideas, events, and people are developed over multiple texts. To do this, you'll likely have to put information together across texts about the idea, event, or person you're tracking. A person might be introduced in one text and then further developed in another text."

Prioritizing Time with Texts You Can Read

Remind students of what they've learned about choosing texts they can read. Channel them to read aloud the text they're currently holding to assess whether they can read that text independently.

"Readers, I want to remind you of something super-important. All the hard work that you're doing to get smarter about your topic won't amount to anything if you're holding texts you can't read really smoothly. There's a group of reading researchers who study kids' reading for a living, and they found that in order for kids to learn something from a text, they need to be reading texts where they can read at least ninety-five out of every one hundred words. (Some researchers think that number should be even higher!) And, they said kids need to be reading texts they can read smoothly, where it sounds like they're talking, and that kids need to read texts they can understand.

"Will you pull out the text you're reading right now? Give that text a quick test by reading a bit of it aloud. Can you read most of the words? Can you read it smoothly? Can you understand what it means? If you can say, 'Yes!' to all those questions, the text is probably just right for you. If not, you'll want to save that text for a little later and look for a text that's easier for you to read right now. I'll give you about two minutes to try this out."

While students read a bit of their text aloud, I moved around the room, especially checking in with students reading below grade level. I celebrated when students noticed a text was too hard and set it aside.

Transition students into their first conversations with their research groups. Observe groups as they work to note which groups transfer their thinking and talking work from Bend I.

"As you dive into your first conversation with your research group, draw on all you know about working in book clubs to help you talk about your new topic. Just remember to talk across all the texts you've read, instead of just one."

As groups talked, I moved from group to group, taking note of how the new groups were working together and what skills they had transferred over from their book-club conversations in Bend I.

DRAWING ON ALL YOUR KNOW AS YOU READ

Tonight, spend thirty to forty minutes reading about your new topic. You can read books and articles from school, or you can do some quick research to find other texts on your topic to read. As you read, draw on everything you learned about reading nonfiction chapter books to help you read your new nonfiction texts well. I'm sending you home with a copy of our chart that you can reference as you read. Take a few minutes to jot about the reading you do, making sure to jot central ideas and not just details.

And make sure you especially work on the goal you set a few days ago!

Summarizing Complex Texts

MINILESSON

CONNECTION

Emphasize the importance of holding on to and understanding one text when reading additional texts on the same topic.

"Readers, last night you read on about your new topic. This morning, some of you told me about the articles and books you read and your enthusiasm was contagious. But as I listened, I noticed something. While you recalled some interesting *details* from across your reading, you didn't have a sense of the *whole* of each text. I'm not surprised—it's hard to hold on to the whole when you're reading a lot of texts in a short time.

"But here's the deal: now that you're reading and thinking about not just *one* longer book at a time, like you did earlier in the unit, but lots of shorter texts, one after another, it's essential that you hold on to the gist of each text as you tackle the next. You have to be sure you understand what one text is teaching on your topic, so that you can add that information to what you learn in the next text you read, and the one after that. You need to be able to hold the contents of each text you read in your mind as you read on."

❖ **Name the teaching point.**

"Today I want to teach you that one way to hold on to any text is to summarize it. To do this, it helps to read a chunk of text thinking, 'What's most essential here?' and then to reduce the text to just the most essential points. Usually that includes the central and main ideas and a few of the most important details."

TEACHING AND ACTIVE ENGAGEMENT

Distribute a chunk of a familiar text to students. Channel partners to read the text thinking, "What's most essential here?" and to generate the text's central idea.

"Since you're reading across so many texts, it won't be possible to hold on to every single tiny detail in each of the texts. Instead, it helps to summarize a text, to boil it down to the most essential points, and then to say those back so that you can hold on to the major things the text is teaching.

"Let's try this together. Today's minilesson will feel more like a boot camp, and I'll coach you through one set of steps readers can take to create a strong summary. To start, it helps to read a chunk of text thinking, 'What's most essential here?' so as to name the central idea in the text. I thought we could reread the section we read yesterday from Alessandra Potenza's article, 'The Battle Over GMOs.' I'll give you and your partner a copy, and then will you get started reading it? Work together to figure out what's most essential in the text, what a central idea might be."

The Battle Over GMOs

Are GMOs the answer to feeding a hungry world, or Frankenfoods that put the environment—and us—at risk?

by Alessandra Potenza / February 8, 2016

Thousands of people recently took to the streets in 400 cities worldwide. The cause of their anger? Not oppressive governments, unemployment, or income inequality, but apples that don't brown when sliced and corn that's bred to fight off insects. In short, GMOs—genetically modified organisms.

In Los Angeles, protesters chanted, "Hell no GMO!" In Strasbourg, France, demonstrators held a minute of silence in front of the European Parliament. And in Rio de Janeiro, Brazil, people accused GMO producers of "bioterrorism."

GMOs are organisms whose DNA has been combined with a gene from an unrelated species to produce a desired trait. Some crops are genetically modified to survive herbicide sprays that kill weeds. Others are engineered to be more nutritious: A pink pineapple awaiting U.S. government approval has the same antioxidant that makes tomatoes red and may help prevent cancer. In November, the U.S. Food and Drug Administration approved the first genetically modified animal: a salmon engineered to grow to market size in about half the time as a regular salmon.

Provisioning students with a familiar text frees them up to practice higher-level summarizing work because they have already had a chance to read the text and make sense of what's happening. Previewing the text with students is a helpful scaffold whenever you feel the text or skill work might be too challenging.

But GMOs haven't been popular lately. Only 37 percent of Americans think they're safe to eat, according to the Pew Research Center. McDonald's recently refused to use a new genetically modified potato that produces less of a cancer-causing chemical when fried. Chipotle dropped GMOs from its U.S. offerings. And General Mills stopped using GMOs in original Cheerios after a yearlong campaign by environmentalists.

'I Don't Think We Know Enough'

While some see GMOs as Frankenfoods that hurt the environment, and us, others see them as the most promising solution to feeding the world's population, which is expected to skyrocket from 7 billion today to 10 billion by 2050. The government agencies regulating GMOs in the U.S. say they're safe. But some scientists and consumers argue that GMOs haven't been around long enough for us to know their long-term health effects.

"We're putting genes into crops that have never been in the food supply before," says Doug Gurian-Sherman, a scientist at the Center for Food Safety, a nonprofit organization opposing GMOs. "I don't think we know enough."

"Talk with your partner. What might be a central idea of the text?"

Pause students to name out a possible central idea of the text. Coach students as they reread, identifying the author's main ideas. Then, pause to name out the main ideas in the text.

"I hear a lot of you saying that a central idea could be that people feel very different ways about GMOs. Now that you've got a central idea in mind, it helps to determine the main points the author is making about this, the main ideas. With your partner, will you reread, and name out some of the main ideas the text is teaching that fit with the central idea? If you come up with four or five, it will help to rank them to determine which main ideas are *most* advanced in this section of the text, because those are the ones you'll want to include in your summary." I listened while students talked.

"Let me say back what I heard. So, you started with a central idea, and now you've got a few of the main points the text makes, the main ideas. I captured some of your points here."

Central idea: People feel very different ways about GMOs.
- Many people think GMOs are harmful.
- Some think GMOs can solve world problems.

Channel students to write-in-the-air their own version of a summary of the text. Listen as partners talk, and then share out one version of a proficient summary with the class.

"Now that you've got the author's central idea and main ideas, it's time to write a summary of the text in the air. It will sound like a short paragraph, where you name the author's central idea and the main points—the main ideas—that back it up. I'll listen in as you try writing it in the air with your partner, being sure to stay close to what the author is actually teaching, not to what you think about GMOs." I listened as students shared their summaries with their partners.

Summarizing is high-level work. Here, you break down the complicated work step-by-step and coach students through it.

When you ask students to write-in-the-air, listen for them to say aloud the exact same words they would write on paper. If you hear students saying "Well, first I would tell the main idea," pause them to give feedback and then have them try writing-in-the-air again.

"Let me share out one of the summaries I heard. Will you particularly try to notice how the reader mentions the author in the summary, and will you see if your summary matches? I heard you saying, 'The author teaches that people feel different ways about GMOs. She begins by explaining that many people think GMOs are harmful to people and the environment. Then, she goes on to say that others think GMOs can end world hunger.'"

Debrief. Name out the steps students just went through to create a concise summary, and add the new learning to the anchor chart.

"Readers, do you see how the summary starts by naming the author's central idea? Then, you state the main ideas that fit with the central idea. It helps to use some transitional phrases to link different parts of the summaries together, like 'the author explains that . . .' and "the author goes on to say that . . .' Let me add this to our anchor chart."

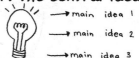

Create a brief summary of the text.

- ◆ Ask, "What's the author's central idea?"

- ◆ Determine main ideas that support the central idea.
  → main idea 1
  → main idea 2
  → main idea 3

- ◆ Say back the central and main ideas in a short paragraph.

If your students need support holding onto the steps readers go through as they summarize, you might distribute small copies of this chart.

ANCHOR CHART

To Research a New Topic . . .

- Preview texts to identify repeating subtopics.
- Build up a bit of background knowledge quickly.
  - Sequence your texts. Start with easier texts–even videos!
  - Teach others what you're learning.
- **Create a brief summary of the text.**
  - **Ask, "What's the author's central idea?"**
  - **Determine main ideas that support the central idea.**
  - **Say back the central and main ideas in a short paragraph.**

Craft a brief summary.

Central Idea

LINK

Emphasize that summarizing can help students to better understand what they are reading. Channel students to write a summary of at least one chunk of their text by the end of the workshop.

"The work you just did summarizing is really critical work to do whenever you're reading, especially in longer texts like these. It helps you to hold on to the essential points of what you're learning and to really understand the author's main points.

"You'll probably pause to summarize often as you're reading today. Mostly, you'll do this in your mind when you finish an article or a section in a longer informational text, but will you pause at least once today to jot down a summary of one text in your notebook? You'll use these summaries with your research group during the share."

Predictable Work to Help Students with Summarizing

WORKING WITH STUDENTS in schools around the world, we've identified several predictable problems that arise when students are summarizing. Here, we outline a few predictable problems and possible teaching points to support students facing those predictable problems. As you confer and pull small groups today, be on the lookout for students who need support in these areas, and then teach responsively.

Students have summaries that include too many main ideas.

You might see students who are struggling to boil a text down to its essentials. Often, this is because students might have listed every possible main idea that's taught in a section of the text without prioritizing which main ideas are most important to include in a summary of the text. If this is the case, you might teach students to look across all the main ideas they've generated and think, "Of all the main ideas this text is teaching, which are *most* taught in the text?" Then, they can rank their main ideas from the main idea that is *most* taught in this section of the text to the main idea that is *least* taught.

To demonstrate using "The Battle Over GMOs" as an example, you could list out the following main ideas:

- Lots of people have protested GMOs.
- GMOs are designed to create a desired trait.
- GMOs can make a food more nutritious.
- Many people are angry about GMOs.
- Some people think GMOs are safe.
- Some people think GMOs can feed the world's population.

Then, you could recruit students to help you quickly rank those main ideas to determine which are most developed in the text. After that, students could return to their summaries and rank their main ideas to determine which were most taught in the text.

Students are confusing details with main ideas.

Other students' summaries might become lengthy because they are confusing main ideas with supporting details. You might notice that they've listed "GMOs are designed to create a desired trait" as one main idea and "A genetically modified salmon can grow large quickly" as another main idea. To help students see that they've listed main ideas and details, you might teach them to reread their possible main ideas, thinking, "Does this fit with/support/elaborate on one of the other ideas?" If so, it's likely a detail that's being given in support of a main idea. Coach them as they reread their main ideas to see if they fit and revise their summaries to include any main ideas that are really details.

The author is absent from the summary.

Other students might be creating a solid summary of the text, but omit any mention of the author from their summary. Naming the author across the summary can help the reader keep his or her opinion separate from the information in the text. If you notice several students who have summarized the text without mentioning the author, you might gather those students together and provide them with a list of sentence starters they can weave into their summary.

Acknowledge the Author in Your Summary

▸ The author teaches…

▸ According to the author…

▸ The author explains/claims/describes…

▸ The author begins/ends by…

Self-Assessing Summaries and Setting Goals

Explain that students can use the anchor chart in multiple ways: to make plans for reading work, to self-assess, and to set goals. Set students up to self-assess their summaries and set goals.

"Our charts are pretty helpful right? So far in this unit, you've been using the anchor charts to make plans for the reading work you'll do at home and at school and to self-assess the work you've already done and to set goals.

"Right now, will you and your partner use the 'Create a brief summary of the text' portion of our anchor chart to help you assess your summaries and set goals for what you can work on moving forward? For instance, you might hold your summary against each bullet, asking, 'Does my summary capture what's most essential, the central idea? Did I determine the main ideas? Did I say them in a short paragraph?' Take note of what you've done and jot a goal for yourself in the future."

Connecting communites, culture, and classrooms

(Central idea)

· Kids are able to make a difference if they put their mind to it.
↳ Anthony Leanne : Heavenly Hats
↳ Brittany Clifford: Fuzzy Feet
↳ Rob and Brittany Bergqvist: Cell Phones for Soldiers
↳ Elizabeth Singleton : Donating Dictionaries

In this article, the author claims about how kids can make a difference if they put their mind to it. She begins explaining about how Anthony Leanne, Brittany Clifford, Rob and Brittany Bergqvist, and Elizabeth Singleton made a difference because they wanted to. She goes on by saying, "Even a spark can turn into a flame if you blow on it."

FIG. 10–1 Erica crafts a summary that includes a central idea and supports.

SESSION 10 HOMEWORK

PAUSE TO SUMMARIZE AS YOU READ

Readers, in class today, you used our anchor chart to self-assess your summary and set goals for yourself moving forward. Tonight, in addition to reading on about your topic, will you pause regularly to summarize? Most of the time, you can do that summarizing work in your mind, but will you jot a quick summary of at least two of your texts (or two parts of a longer text) so you can hold on to the big things those texts taught? I'll send our "To Research a New Topic . . ." anchor chart home so you can recall everything readers do as they summarize.

Synthesizing across Texts

IN THIS SESSION

TODAY YOU'LL teach students that non-fiction readers regularly synthesize across texts on a topic. When they read new texts, they consider how the information they are learning fits with, extends, or contradicts what they have read earlier.

TODAY YOUR STUDENTS will read several articles or texts on their topic and take notes that allow them to synthesize what they're learning across texts, perhaps by dividing their notes into subtopics, or by developing another note-taking system.

GETTING READY

✔ Print out copies of the "What Are GMOs?" notes for each student. Students will practice synthesizing new information into these notes (see Teaching and Active Engagement).

✔ Cue the "Seeing Red: The Flavr Savr Tomato" video to play from 1:00 to 5:11. A link to the video is available in the online resources (see Teaching and Active Engagement).

✔ Prepare to add to the "To Research a New Topic . . ." anchor chart (see Teaching and Active Engagement and Link).

✔ Ensure that students have access to the "To Make the Most of Your Nonfiction Texts" anchor chart from Session 9 (see Link).

✔ Print out copies of the "To Synthesize across Texts" mini-chart to support students' conversations about multiple texts (see Conferring and Small-Group Work).

✔ Mark a page in your reader's notebook that shows the messy work of synthesizing texts in your notes (see Conferring and Small-Group Work).

MINILESSON

CONNECTION

Set students up to tour one another through their homework. Point out patterns you notice in their note-taking, and offer them a tip to make their note-taking stronger.

"As soon as you get to the meeting area, tour your partner through the homework you did over the last few nights." While students briefly shared, I moved around the meeting area, taking note of whose homework was completed and observing common characteristics of their note-taking.

"As I look across your notebooks, I'm noticing the quick jots you did these past few nights almost all have something in common. They're all organized by text. That is, your notes about the first article you read are on one page, and then your notes on the next article start on the next page. It feels like you're thinking about each article on its own, in isolation.

"But whenever you read multiple texts on a topic, it helps to consider how all the information you're learning fits together. I've been doing something different with my notes that helps fit all the information I'm learning together, and I thought I could teach you about it."

✣ **Name the teaching point.**

"Today I want to teach you that nonfiction readers synthesize their previous learning with their new learning to form new insights. As they read new texts on their topic, they ask, 'Does this fit with, extend, or contradict what I've read earlier?' Then, they incorporate what they learned into their notes."

TEACHING AND ACTIVE ENGAGEMENT

Distribute brief notes and have students familiarize themselves with the notes. Rally students to help you synthesize learning between familiar texts and a video.

I passed out a brief sheet of notes to each student and said, "Here are some of the notes I've jotted about the articles we've been reading. Take a minute to familiarize yourself with the notes. Notice that I set my notes up by subtopic, not by text? I set up different sections based on the subtopics we identified on Day One, and then I sorted the information I learned under the different headings."

What Are GMOs?

- Genes—do different things to make organisms
- Genetic engineering—building something with genes
- Splicing—snipping genes out of one organism and putting them in another
- GMOs—genetically modified organisms; gene from another species added to their DNA

Disagreements around GMOs

- Protests in the streets
- 37% of Americans think GMOs are safe (Pew Research Center)
- McDonald's pulled GMO potatoes

Kinds of GMOs

- Cancer-fighting foods
- Foods that grow quickly (salmon)
- Foods that survive pesticides
- 90% of corn is modified

If you want to lift the level of the notes you provision students with, you could add in central ideas you've learned about each topic. That way, when students revise the notes, they'll have to determine which category the new information fits with and revise the central ideas to account for that new information.

After students had thirty seconds to read through, I continued. "So, let's try this. We'll study a new text—a video about the Flavr Savr tomato. Instead of creating a brand-new page of notes, we'll add the new information we're learning to the existing notes."

Pause the video along the way, and ask students to consider whether the new information they are learning fits with, extends, or contradicts their earlier learning.

I cued the video to 1:00 and hit play. At 2:35, I paused the video and said, "Talk with your partner. How does the new information you heard fit with, extend, or contradict what we've already learned about genetic engineering?"

I called students back to summarize, touching the relevant portions of my notes as I talked. "So far it seems like what we're learning mostly fits with what we already knew. You said the video is discussing different reasons why people make GMOs, and maybe it's extending what we know by introducing a new reason for making a GMO, to keep food fresh longer.

"Let's keep watching, alert for how this new text fits with, extends, or contradicts what we've read so far." I hit play, and we powered through the video until around the 5:11 mark.

Recruit students to briefly revise the shared notes to incorporate what they learned.

"Work with your partner to determine how this new text fits with, extends, or contradicts what we've already read."

Many students shared that this portion of the video felt different from other information they'd read about GMOs. The media and public seemed excited about the Flavr Savr tomato. People didn't seem concerned about any possible negative effects.

After a minute, I voiced over, "With your partner, revise the shared notes to incorporate only the most critical parts of what you just heard. You might add new information in with arrows where it belongs or revise parts that you know now are inaccurate."

I asked one partnership to share their revisions to the notes with the class. They said, "We thought some of the information extended what we knew about disagreements around GMOs because most articles so far have talked about people who dislike GMOs, and this one talked about how there was a really positive reaction to the tomatoes, so we added to the disagreements around GMOs category. And we also heard about another kind of GMO, so we added that to the list."

What Are GMOs?

- Genes—do different things to make organisms

- Genetic engineering—building something with genes

- Splicing—snipping genes out of one organism and putting them in another

- GMOs—genetically modified organisms; gene from another species added to their DNA

Disagreements Around GMOs
- Inventors had no idea what they were doing at the start (no expertise in agriculture)
- Protests in the streets

- 37 percent of Americans think GMOs are safe (Pew Research Center)

- McDonald's pulled GMO potatoes
- They did not need FDA Approvement but got it anyway to attract the general public
- when released some were skeptical of the chemicals it may have

Kinds of GMOs

- Cancer-fighting foods

- Foods that grow quickly (salmon)

- Foods that survive pesticides

- 90 percent of corn is modified
- Foods that ripen quicker
- More shelf time (lasts longer)

FIG. 11–1 Will and Molly revise the notes to incorporate their new learning.

What Are GMOs?

- Genes—do different things to make organisms
- Genetic engineering—building something with genes
- Splicing—snipping genes out of one organism and putting them in another
- GMOs—genetically modified organisms; gene from another species added to their DNA

Disagreements around GMOs

- Protests in the streets
- 37% of Americans think GMOs are safe (Pew Research Center)
- McDonald's pulled GMO potatoes
- **First GMO product = tomato; people LOVED it; sold for 2x the money**

Kinds of GMOs

- Cancer-fighting foods
- Foods that grow quickly (salmon)
- Foods that survive pesticides
- 90% of corn is modified
- **Foods that stay fresh longer (Flavr Savr Tomato)**

Debrief, restating the teaching point. Add the new point to the anchor chart.

"If we had started note-taking on a whole new page, we would have wasted valuable reading time rewriting things we learned about in other texts. Instead, we synthesized our previous learning with our new learning, looking for ways the new information fit with, extended, or contradicted what we'd read earlier. Then, we added only critical new information to our notes."

LINK

Challenge students to review their writing and set up files in their notebooks for note-taking. Send them off to read with a reminder to draw on all they know as nonfiction readers.

"Before you start reading today, get yourself set up to take notes that allow you to synthesize what you're learning across texts. You might divide your notes into subtopics, like I did, jot possible central ideas across the tops of your notebook pages, or develop another note-taking system. And of course, remember to use the 'To Research a New Topic' anchor chart and the 'To Make the Most of Your Nonfiction Texts . . .' anchor chart to help you draw on all you know as a nonfiction reader. Off you go!"

ANCHOR CHART

To Research a New Topic . . .

- Preview texts to identify repeating subtopics.
- Build up a bit of background knowledge quickly.
  - Sequence your texts. Start with easier texts—even videos!
  - Teach others what you're learning.
- Create a brief summary of the text.
  - Ask, "What's the author's central idea?"
  - Determine main ideas that support the central idea.
  - Say back the central and main ideas in a short paragraph.
- **Synthesize across texts.**
  - **Fit with?**
  - **Extends?**
  - **Contradicts?**

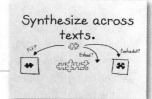

Synthesize across texts.

Supporting the Complex Work of Synthesizing across Texts

STUDENTS ARE IN THEIR FOURTH DAY of reading texts on their text set. You'll want to look to see that students have read across several texts, both articles and trade books.

Today, you might choose to support students in synthesizing across texts, either in one-on-one conferences or in small groups. Below you'll find suggestions for how you can support cross-text synthesis by teaching into students' reading, note-taking, and research group conversations. If you find that nearly all of the class could benefit from any of the following teaching points, you might tuck some of the instruction into the share at the end of the session.

To Synthesize Across Texts...

AND...
BUT...

- "This text fits with what you said because..."

- "This text gives more support for..."

- "This text extends what you said..."

- "This text says something different..."

- "This text contradicts what you said..."

If you notice . . .	Then you might teach . . .
Students are not taking into account all parts of the text, including text features, as they read and as they consider central ideas.	"Readers, I'm seeing some of you just skip over the text features in your texts. What I want to teach you is that you need to take time to study those text features because authors have included them for a reason. You can study each one closely asking, 'What does this text feature teach? And, how exactly does it fit with the central ideas in the text?' This work will give you a deeper idea of the text features *and* of the central ideas in the text."
Students are forming initial ideas about their topic and then holding those ideas tightly as they read on. It's as if they only look for evidence that confirms their ideas, and they disregard evidence that might lead them to revise their thinking.	"Remember how when you were reading across your nonfiction chapter books, you formed initial ideas of what the text was teaching and then as you read on, you revised the central ideas in light of the new information you gathered? Even though the texts in your text set are shorter, you still have to do that same work as you read across your topic. You read one text on your topic, and you get an initial sense of the central ideas that are true for your topic. Then, as you read across other texts, you have to hold those initial ideas loosely and be ready to revise your thinking about the central ideas as you read on. "Will you try this right now? Start by reminding yourself of the central ideas that you already think are true for your topic, and then read on, alert to information that might lead you to revise your thinking about those central ideas. Get to it!"

If you notice . . .	Then you might teach . . .
Students organize their notes by text, rather than by subtopic. In other words, they aren't synthesizing information across texts in their notes.	"Nonfiction researchers often set up different files in their notebook to collect notes, rather than starting a new page of notes each time they read a new text. Those files often represent the different subtopics they are researching. Then, they can file the new information they learn into the subtopic where it most belongs. "Think about your topic. What subtopics show up repeatedly that should have their own sections in your notebook? Right here, right now, create new note-taking pages for those subtopics."
Students are jotting notes based on subtopic, but they add new notes to the bottom of each subtopic instead of thinking about where precisely those notes should fit.	"Let me give you a tip. Synthesis is messy work. It's not enough to add notes to the bottom of a page. Instead, when you're synthesizing between texts, sometimes you have to cross parts out that are no longer true. Sometimes you have to add arrows to show where exactly the new information you're learning belongs, what other information it fits with." I showed a sample page from my notebook that captured this work. "Ready to give this a try? Which subtopic do you want to start with? Look across the notes you already have, and see if you need to make any revisions. What needs to be crossed out, rearranged, to show how parts fit together?" "As you read forward, keep doing this work as you read!"
In their research groups, students are talking about only one text at a time, rather than drawing upon multiple texts to grow their conversations. There are no points of comparison or contrast drawn between the texts.	"I'm listening to your talk, and it sounds like you're doing the same thing some of you were doing in your notebooks. You're talking about one text and then another text and then a third text all in isolation, instead of talking about how the information in the different texts works together. "There are a few prompts that can especially support you in synthesizing across texts as you talk." **To Synthesize across Texts:** • "This text fits with what you said because . . ." • "This text gives more support for . . ." • "This text extends what you said . . ." • "This text said something different . . ." • "This text contradicts what you said . . ." "Will you restart your conversation, this time pushing yourselves to talk *across* texts? Use these prompts to help you."

Synthesizing across Texts as You Talk

Set research groups up to synthesize across texts as they talk. Move from group to group, observing and coaching in.

"Let me give you a tip before you meet in your research groups. Synthesizing information across texts isn't just work that you do as you read and take notes. It's also work you do as you talk. As you talk in your clubs, listen for how the new information your group mates share fits with, extends, or contradicts what you read. It will be particularly interesting to talk about points of contradiction, if you find any.

"Launch into your conversations. After one person shares, be sure to think, 'How does this fit with, extend, or contradict what I read?'"

I moved from group to group, coaching in as the groups talked. To one group, I said, "You've named how the two texts are different. Now, go into the text and prove it! Pull out specific parts that make your point."

To another group, I coached, "I hear you saying, 'This fits . . .' and 'This fits . . .' Even texts that teach about the same general thing often make slightly different points about it. Push yourself to consider whether your texts are precisely the same or a little bit different."

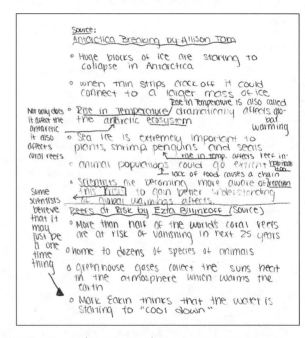

FIG. 11–2   Dabney revises her notes to incorporate information from a second text on the same topic.

SESSION 11 HOMEWORK

SYNTHESIZING ACROSS TEXTS ON YOUR TOPIC

Tonight, as you read, don't think about each of your texts in isolation. Instead, consider how each new text adds to or changes what you've already learned. Ask yourself, "Does this fit with other things I've read? Does this extend my thinking? Does it contradict my thinking?" Use your note-taking system to record some of the new information you're learning and to show how it fits with what you already know.

Dealing with Tricky Parts

Reading Outside the Text to Help You Comprehend Inside

GETTING READY

✓ Select an article that includes some difficult information. We use "The Battle Over GMOs" by Alessandra Potenza (see Teaching and Active Engagement). 👏

✓ Choose a related website to show students how you turn to an explanatory text for help. We use http://encyclopedia.kids.net.au/page/he/Herbicide. A link to this site is available in the online resources (see Teaching). 👏

✓ Ask students to bring their cell phones with them to the meeting area, so they can do some quick research. Groups of students can share a device. If you can't manage access to technology in the meeting area, ask the kids to consider what they could search (see Active Engagement).

✓ Add to the "To Research a New Topic . . ." anchor chart (see Link). 👏

✓ Provide the "To Make the Most of Your Nonfiction Texts" anchor chart (see Link) 👏

✓ Provide a mini version of the "To Research a New Topic . . ." anchor chart (see Homework). 👏

IN THIS SESSION

TODAY YOU'LL teach students that readers often turn to outside resources to deepen their comprehension of tricky parts of their nonfiction books. Readers might turn to easier texts, explanatory texts, or texts that provide follow-up information.

TODAY YOUR STUDENTS will continue reading their text sets, going outside of the text to do quick research as needed to clear up any confusion.

MINILESSON

CONNECTION

Explain to students that as nonfiction texts become complex, authors often expect an expert reader.

"The background knowledge you've started building up is definitely helpful. It lets you understand more in your texts than you might have if you had gone into the tougher texts cold.

"Here's the thing, though. You know the nonfiction texts you're reading now are becoming more complex. One of the ways they're getting tricky is that many of these texts expect an expert reader. Sometimes this means that the text expects you to know a lot of background information already. At other times, it means that the author will use unfamiliar words and mention concepts that are totally critical to understanding the text, but they won't give you any support at all to figure out what those critical but tricky words mean.

"Luckily, there are some things you can do when you get to these tricky parts in the text."

❧ **Name the teaching point.**

"Today I want to teach you that once you're in a text, you sometimes need to go outside of it to deepen your comprehension of tricky parts. Specifically, it can help to turn to texts that might be easier, explanatory, or provide follow-up information that's missing in the text."

TEACHING

Demonstrate how you read an article alert for parts where the author expects an expert reader. Identify a tricky part, and then show how you turn to an outside resource for clarity.

"The strongest nonfiction readers are willing to go outside of the text they're reading to help them make sense of tricky parts. Going outside the text, even if it's just for a minute or two, can dramatically increase your understanding of a confusing part.

"Let's read a bit on in 'The Battle Over GMOs,' on the lookout for places where the author expects an expert reader and we might need to go outside the text to get information." I projected the article and began reading aloud from where we left off earlier.

> The first GMO, a tomato that ripened without softening, was sold in the U.S. in 1994.

"So far so good, right? Quick, remind your partner of the background knowledge you already have that fits with what we're learning." I listened in as students discussed the Flavr Savr tomato.

> (It was later taken off the market.) In 1996, soybeans and corn that resist herbicides and kill pests were introduced. Both crops proved immediately popular with farmers. Today 94 percent of soybeans and 93 percent of corn planted in the U.S. is genetically altered—and most of it ends up in processed foods.

"Hmm, . . . I feel like the author is expecting an expert reader here. She just mentioned herbicides, but I'm not really sure what they are. Maybe I could find a text that explains what herbicides are. Let's try searching for super-easy articles on herbicides on the internet."

I pulled up a new search, typed in "what are herbicides? for kids" and hit enter. "Let me quickly find a search result that looks informative. What about this one from Kids Net?" I clicked on it, and started scrolling through the page.

"Okay, so this says that herbicides are things used to kill unwanted plants. It sounds like some herbicides only kill certain plants, and other herbicides kill *all* plants they touch. Wow!"

Return to the article and demonstrate how you fit the new information you learned with the information in the text.

"Now that I've got a tiny bit more knowledge, I can reread the confusing part of the text and see if I understand more. Here goes: 'In 1996, soybeans and corn that resist herbicides and kill pests were introduced.' I guess it's saying that soybeans and corn that can't be killed by herbicides were created, which would be important because then farmers could use herbicides to kill weeds, but wouldn't have to worry about the herbicides killing the soybeans or corn."

Name out the transferable strategies you used when you encountered a tricky part.

"So, do you see how once you're inside a text, sometimes you need to go outside of it to make sense of it? You can go outside a text quickly, maybe doing some quick Internet research, talking to an expert, or watching a video. Of course, you can draw upon other texts in your text set that might help. Then, when you go back inside the text and reread, usually you find you're able to understand more."

ACTIVE ENGAGEMENT

Rally students to try out the strategy as you read on. Encourage students to generate their own point of confusion, but have one ready to point out to students as needed.

"Will you give this a try with another part of 'The Battle Over GMOs'? I'll display it, and will you read through on the lookout for a part that's confusing, a part where you might want to go outside the text for more information? Or, if you feel like you're a total expert, look for a part newbies might find confusing."

A Boon to Farmers?

Carrière argues that bug-killing crops are beneficial because they reduce the use of insecticides, which can harm people and the environment. (Between 1996 and 2011, bug-killing corn reduced insecticide use in corn production by 45 percent worldwide.) Developing crops that can survive dry climates, others say, could help us grow food as climate change makes the planet more prone to droughts. Such crops could make a difference for drought-stricken states like California.

"Name for your partner what part feels tricky and why." I gave students just a moment to talk.

"I heard you naming out a bunch of parts that could be tricky. Listen if you didn't find one, and choose one of these to work with. Some of you said you weren't sure what insecticides were, and you want to look that up. Some of you want to research more about how these crops could help drought-stricken states. And some of you said you want to do more research about droughts, to really understand what they are."

When you notice a point of confusion, study an outside text to clear up that confusion, and then return back to the original text to demonstrate for students another way readers can synthesize across texts. This is work you began in Session 11 but students will benefit from repeated exposure. It's critical that you help students see how the outside resource you studied boosts your understanding of the initial text.

Coach students as they quickly turn to outside resources—via their cell phones or computers—to clear up their confusions.

"Right now, will you do something smart to clear up that confusion? Pull out your cell phones and computers. Pull up an Internet browser and search what you're wondering, look up a definition, do some quick research. You've got two minutes right now to turn to outside resources."

Channel students to reread the text and notice ways in which their comprehension has improved.

"All right, phones away! Equipped with that research you just did, dive back into the text, and see if you can comprehend that part of the text even better now. You should be able to understand more now than you did a few minutes ago."

If you can't manage access to technology in the meeting area, you might instead invite students to consider what search terms they could enter to clear up their confusion. If you can project an internet browser, you might enter one of the suggested search terms for the class so they can get practice scanning the results and making decisions about what to study.

LINK

Link today's teaching point to the work students have done during previous sessions in the unit. Set students up to reflect on what they want to work on while they read today.

"Remember that whenever a text you're reading gets confusing, going outside of the text to do a bit of quick research can really help. You can look online for texts, talk to people who can help you clear up your confusions and make sense of what's missing in the text, or look for answers in the texts in your text set." I added to the "To Research a New Topic . . . anchor chart.

"Of course, you know lots of work you can do as a reader, so this won't be the only thing you work on today. You'll probably only need to do this once or twice as you read, so will you take a minute to look over our anchor charts, think about what you've been working on lately and what you might need to work more on, and then give me a thumbs up when you have a plan?" I referenced the "To Make the Most of Your Nonfiction ~~Chapter Books~~ Texts" chart and the "To Research a New Topic . . ." chart.

"Off you go to get started!"

ANCHOR CHART

To Research a New Topic . . .

- Preview texts to identify repeating subtopics.
- Build up a bit of background knowledge quickly.
  - Sequence your texts. Start with easier texts—even videos!
  - Teach others what you're learning.
- Create a brief summary of the text.
  - Ask, "What's the author's central idea?"
  - Determine main ideas that support the central idea.
  - Say back the central and main ideas in a short paragraph.
- Synthesize across texts.
  - Fit with?
  - Extends?
  - Contradicts?
- **Turn to outside resources to clear up confusion.**

Turn to outside resources to clear up confusions.

Using a Partner to Make Sense of Harder Parts of Nonfiction Texts

IT MATTERS that your students are holding texts that they can read with at least 95% accuracy, as well as with fluency and comprehension. The priority here is that students grow as readers, not that they become experts on GMOs or child soldiers or any other particular topic, and holding texts they can read with fluency, with essential comprehension, is central to this goal. Occasionally, readers will find it hard to read brief passages embedded within a text, but the text itself is mostly accessible, and you'll want to teach kids how to work through those hard parts. But, if the majority of the text feels hard, or if kids can't figure out one word in ten within the text, that text is likely too difficult and should be swapped for another text. The reader might be able to return to it later, once they've built up some background knowledge.

If you see students getting sidetracked by the dense passages in their texts, you might gather these students, ideally with a partner from their research group, and teach a small group on using a partner to make sense of tricky parts.

To start, you might explain why you gathered students together and name the teaching point. "You're encountering confusing passages in your texts, and sometimes, going outside the text to get more information doesn't clear up your confusion. In those situations, it can help to use a partner to help you make sense of the tricky part. You can read the passage together a bit at a time, talking along the way to teach each other what you're learning."

To keep your teaching brief, you might share an example of what you mean. You might say, "In college, the reading expectations are pretty high. When I was in college, I got a lot of reading assignments that seemed pretty far over my head. Can I tell you what I did, and you can see if what I did might help you? When I was faced with a tricky article or book, I would meet with a friend from class so we could help each other get through it. We'd start by breaking the text into small, manageable chunks. After that, we read each chunk and tried to teach each other what we were learning. We used as many of the important words as we could while we taught. By the end, we both understood that tricky part better than we had before."

Then, channel students to try this in their own texts. You might say, "Will you and your partner give this a try? Start by going back to a tricky passage you recently encountered, and try reading little bits of it together, pausing to teach what you're learning along the way."

As students reread and teach, be ready to coach in. Here are a few lean prompts that might be useful as you're coaching students:

- "Reread it again if it doesn't quite make sense."
- "Read just a small chunk, and then stop and teach what you're learning."
- "Use the important words in the text as you teach."
- "Say what you understand *and* what you don't understand."

You might notice a few students who read along without noting tricky passages. It may be that the text is totally accessible or that they have built up enough background knowledge to understand it, or it may be that they are not monitoring for meaning. Be ready to coach in around this. You might say:

- "As you read, ask yourself, 'Does this make total sense?' If not, it's a sign that part is tricky."
- "Pause, and try to say back the main things this part teaches."
- "Think about how that part fits with what you read earlier."

To close the small group, restate your teaching point. Then, link the work students just did to the ongoing work they should be doing as they head off to read.

Collaborating to Build Up Background Knowledge

Rally students to meet in research groups. Explain how collaboration can help you build up more background knowledge than you could independently and to clarify confusion.

"A sure fire way to learn more about *anything* is to get together with other people who are learning about that topic—in this case, the kids in your research group—and share your new knowledge. Likely, you've each learned slightly different things on your topic. For example, in the *Titanic* research group, maybe one of you learned about the problems in the engine room, and another of you learned about how the first-class cabins were decorated, and a third group member learned about the hype before the voyage. Now, you can put all that information together to grow some bigger ideas about the *Titanic*.

"Will you get together and share some of the background knowledge you accumulated through your outside research? Talk about what you understand, and talk also about the parts you're still confused about to see if your team can help you clarify them. Teaching someone else about your learning is a great way to solidify that learning for yourself."

SESSION 12 HOMEWORK

 READING WITH CLARITY

Readers, tonight you'll want to spend thirty to forty minutes researching your topic. I'm sending you home with a copy of our "To Research a New Topic . . ." anchor chart. As you read, draw on all you know about how readers research. Make sure you are synthesizing information across texts as you read, considering how the new information you're learning fits with, extends, or contradicts what you read before.

If you find yourself confused as you read, remember that you can turn to outside resources to clear up that confusion. Do a quick Internet search, look for answers in another article, or phone a friend who might help. Just make sure that after you do some quick research, you dive back into the text you were reading and see if you can understand the text a bit better. Happy researching!

Getting to Know the Lingo of Your Topic

GETTING READY

✔ Prepare to jot the vocabulary words related to the whole-class research topic on Post-its that you can sort on a white board or chart paper (see Connection, Teaching, and Active Engagement).

✔ Create a "Ways to Sort Key Vocabulary" one-day chart (see Active Engagement and Share).

✔ Distribute index cards to each research group for students to collect vocabulary on (see Link).

✔ Prepare to add a new bullet to the "To Research a New Topic . . ." anchor chart (see Link).

✔ Print copies of the "Look ALL Around a Word for Clues" mini-chart to support students in determining the meaning of words in context (see Conferring and Small-Group Work).

✔ Provide copies of the sample word morphology log for students to track word parts (see Conferring and Small-Group Work).

IN THIS SESSION

TODAY YOU'LL teach students that to know a topic well, it helps to study the vocabulary of that topic. They can sort and re-sort the key words, considering how they fit together.

TODAY YOUR STUDENTS will spend most of their work time reading through a volume of texts and drawing on the repertoire of strategies they learned not only in this bend, but also in Bend 1. Along the way they will gather vocabulary words to help them learn the lingo of their topic.

MINILESSON

CONNECTION

Ask students to help you generate a list of words related to the whole-class research topic. Record each word students generate on a Post-it note.

"We've already encountered so many new words and phrases in our study of genetic engineering. I started jotting a few of the words down on Post-it notes." I added Post-it notes with the terms *genetic engineering*, *genes*, and *herbicides* to the board. "With your partner, will you generate a list of other words that are significant to our topic that we should add up here?" As students talked, I jotted the words they mentioned. Soon the board looked like this.

genetic engineering	genes	herbicides	splicing
resistant	trait	organisms	pesticides
GMOs	DNA	protesters	Frankenfoods

"Today I want to teach you that nonfiction readers work to know the vocabulary of their topic, since the vocabulary is intricately linked to the key concepts in the text. One way they do this is by sorting and re-sorting the words of their topic. Then, they talk about the words in different ways, considering ways the words fit together."

TEACHING

Explain why knowing the vocabulary of a topic matters.

"To really know a topic well, you have to have real mastery of the vocabulary of that topic. It's not enough to just know what the important words are, or to simply list them. Instead, you have to be able to use those words flexibly, to sort them and re-sort them, and to talk about them in lots of different ways."

Demonstrate one way you can sort the words into categories. Think aloud about how the key vocabulary in each category fits together.

"Let me show you how I do this. How could I sort these words? Well, I could sort them into words I know really well and words I don't really know. Or, I could use some of the central ideas I've encountered so far to sort them. Maybe I could sort them into words that have to do with physically genetically engineering something and words that have to do with the conflict around GMOs."

I divided the board into two categories, and I labeled each one. Then, I modeled how I sorted the words on Post-its into categories.

"Now, to solidify my understanding of these words, let me take one of these categories—words that have to do with genetically engineering something—and think about how the words fit together." I touched each word as I talked about it. "Okay, so with *genetic engineering*, you're taking the *genes* from one *species*—which is also called an *organism*—that have a certain *trait*, and you put them into another *species* through *splicing*. That's how you make a *GMO*. Sometimes the *GMO* is made to be *resistant* to different chemicals, but they can be made for other reasons.

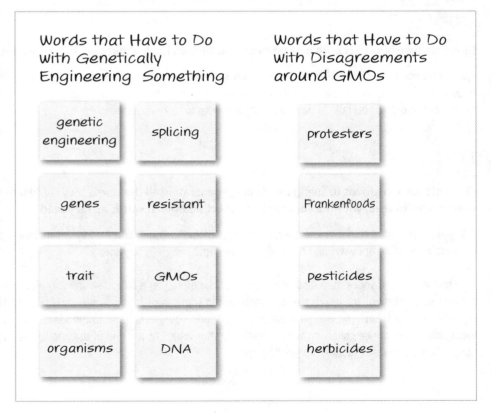

"Do you see how I sorted the words into different categories? Then, I talked across the words to consider how they fit together. I made sure to use each word as I talked."

ACTIVE ENGAGEMENT

Reveal a chart with options for ways to sort key vocabulary words. Then, rally students to choose another way to sort.

I revealed a chart I'd prepared to show students different ways they might sort the vocabulary words of a topic. "Here are a few different ways to sort words to help solidify your understanding of them."

"Let's try one of these together. Do you think you could sort the words into three categories: positive words, neutral words, and negative words?" I added the three categories to the top of the board.

"With your partner, get started sorting the words into these three categories. Name the words you'd put into each category."

Direct partnerships to choose one category and turn and talk about how the words are related.

"Now that you've sorted the words, you're ready for the next step. Will you choose *one* of these categories—positive, neutral, or negative—and talk through why the words you sorted into that category belong in that category? Be sure to use each word as you talk." I gave students a minute to talk while I coached in.

LINK

Channel research groups to spend two minutes generating all the words they can related to their topics. Send students off to read, with the challenge to collect additional words as they read.

"Whenever you want to get to know a topic better, it helps to linger with the key vocabulary of that topic. You can sort the vocabulary different ways and think about how those words fit together.

"I'm giving you and your group a stack of index cards. Before you read today, will you and your group mates take two minutes to generate all the words that are important to your topic? Jot the words you know well and the words you just know a little. Look back through your articles, books, and notes as needed to get ideas. And as you read and research today, will you continue collecting words related to your topic? At the end of reading today, you and your club will be able to sort your words, just like we did together.

Ways to Sort Key Vocabulary

The work of jotting vocabulary words should be quick—just a few minutes. You won't want it to take away from kids' time to read.

"I'll add this work to our anchor chart, so you can keep it in mind along with all else you are doing to learn from your text sets."

ANCHOR CHART

To Research a New Topic . . .

- Preview texts to identify repeating subtopics.
- Build up a bit of background knowledge quickly.
  - Sequence your texts. Start with easier texts—even videos!
  - Teach others what you're learning.
- Create a brief summary of the text.
  - Ask, "What's the author's central idea?"
  - Determine main ideas that support the central idea.
  - Say back the central and main ideas in a short paragraph.
- Synthesize across texts.
  - Fit with?
  - Extends?
  - Contradicts?
- Turn to outside resources to clear up confusions.
- **Become an expert on the topic's lingo.**

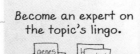

Become an expert on the topic's lingo.

genes
DNA
splicing
pesticide

Helping Students Build Robust Vocabularies

TODAY STUDENTS should be reading across multiple texts on their topic. Keep an eye out for students who are stuck on a single text, and help them make plans to move on to the next text shortly. Make sure students are continuing to draw on the work you've supported across this bend. That is, students should be synthesizing information they are learning across texts, jotting only briefly in response to their reading, and turning to outside resources if they find themselves stumped. If you do not see students doing this work, draw on Conferring and Small-Group Work sections from earlier in the unit for ideas of how to offer support.

In the texts your students are reading now, the hard words they encounter are usually deeply tied to the central ideas in the text. Because of this, students will benefit from not just identifying the new words they're learning, but also from doing some work to determine what those words mean. To support students in building their vocabularies, you might lead a series of small groups that support students in using context, word morphology, and reference materials to determine the meaning of unfamiliar words.

Determining the Meaning of Words in Context

If you see students constantly going to their phones or a computer to look up the meaning of unfamiliar words, you might gather those students together to support them in using context as a clue to determine a word's meaning. You could say, "I see you're doing some outside research to figure out what words mean, and that can definitely be helpful. However, there are actually a *ton* of clues about what words mean already in your texts. Let me share with you some tips that will help you find more of the clues hidden in a text." Then, you could share a mini-chart listing tips for determining the meaning of words in context.

Rather than demonstrating, you might quickly launch students into trying the work. "Read on in your books, alert to words and phrases that are unfamiliar. When you find one, look all around the word for clues. Use the chart to help you. I'll give you some pink Post-it notes. Flag the words you work to determine the meaning of with a Post-it note."

When you see a student reaching for a Post-it note, that's your cue to lean in and do some coaching. Keep your coaching lean. You might say, "Look for clues" or "Check the chart. What other clues could you look for?" or "Try envisioning what's going on. What do you see? Use that to help you." To wrap up your group, you might leave students with a mini-copy of the chart and additional pink Post-it notes so they can continue this work as they read on.

Drawing on Knowledge of Word Morphology to Word Solve

If you have a research group reading about topics related to science, they might benefit from a small group on using word morphology to determine the meaning of unfamiliar words. As Tim Shanahan and other literacy researchers have pointed out, science terms often have Latin and Greek roots (e.g., *carnivore*, *herbivore*, *annual*, *biennial*, *perennial*). Your students' ability to draw on word morphology as a source of information is, of course, limited by their knowledge of word parts. What prefixes, suffixes, and root words do your students know? Have they had any formal experience with word morphology? It's possible they have not. Luckily, there are some common prefixes, suffixes, and root words you might teach your students to provide them an entryway into most words they're trying to break apart.

You can quickly gather a research group and teach them about the most common prefixes and suffixes. To do this, you might give students a tool where they can track word parts. In the online resources, you'll find a sample word morphology log, which features some of the most high-leverage prefixes and suffixes. A few of the most common prefixes (*dis–*, *in–*, *im–*, *il–*, *ir–*, *re–*, and *un–*) account for 89% of the prefixed words in printed school English. Then quickly, you'll want to coach students as they put the tool to use to determine the meaning of unfamiliar words in the text they're reading.

As you coach, you might say, "See if you can divide the word into parts. Which parts are you sure about? Less sure about?" You can coach students to figure out what a part might mean by thinking about words they know that are similar. You could say, "Can you think of other words that have the same word parts?" "Put the meaning of each part together to determine what the word means."

Using Reference Materials to Determine Word Meaning

In texts at these levels, authors often embed technical words without providing the necessary support that would help readers determine a word's precise meaning through context. If you see students lingering too long on particular words, you might lead a small group about turning to reference materials, both print and digital, to determine the meaning of an unfamiliar word.

First, you might gather a group of students and teach them that sometimes their texts won't provide enough support to determine the precise meaning of an unfamiliar word. You could use the article "The Battle Over GMOs" to quickly demonstrate how you can't determine the precise meaning of *bioterrorism* perfectly from context. You might first think aloud about how you used context to determine that the word seems to have a negative connotation. Then, show students how you turn to a dictionary to clarify the definition. For instance, Dictionary.com defines *bioterrorism* as "terrorist acts involving the use of harmful agents or products of biological origin, as in disease-producing microorganisms or toxins."

After a brief demonstration, no more than a minute or two long, invite students to try out the same work, reading until they come to an unfamiliar word or phrase, pausing and using context to make guesses about the word's meaning or connotation, and then turning to a dictionary to clarify the word's definition. Coach students as they use the context as a clue and a dictionary, either print or digital, as a secondary resource.

Sorting and Re-Sorting to Develop a Deeper Understanding of a Topic

Set up research groups to sort and re-sort the words related to their topic. As they sort, coach them to discuss how the words fit together and to add additional words to their collection.

"Your word stacks are growing and growing. When you meet with your research group today, will you use some of your time together to deeply study the words of your topic? Choose one way to sort the words, sort them, and then talk about how the words fit together. Then, start over, and re-sort the words a new way." I gestured to the "Ways to Sort Key Vocabulary" chart. "You might sort based on words that are positive and negative, words that fit under different subtopics, words you know and words you don't know, and more!"

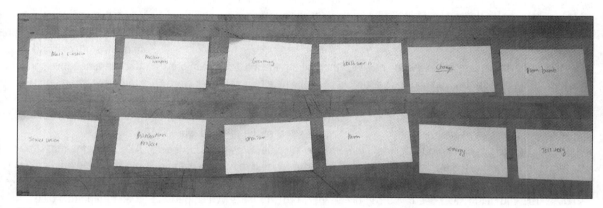

FIG. 13–1 Enver sorts key vocabulary related to atomic bombs chronologically.

USING THE LINGO OF YOUR TOPIC TO LIFT THE LEVEL OF YOUR NOTES

To become an expert in your topic, you have to become an expert in your topic's lingo. To learn an unfamiliar word and add it to your vocabulary, it helps to practice using it right away, and to take some risks with it. One way to do this is to incorporate all the new words and phrases you're learning into your notes. Tonight, aim for your usual reading of about forty minutes. Make sure you read across a few articles and do some brief jotting, and be sure to use the expert words of your topic. If you come across any words or concepts you can't quite grasp, remember that it helps to do some quick research to figure out what those words might mean.

Readers Don't Wait to Do Their Own Thinking

IN THIS SESSION

TODAY YOU'LL teach students that readers of nonfiction don't accept what the authors teach at face value; instead, readers grow their own ideas and develop their own theories about their topics.

TODAY YOUR STUDENTS will work on growing their own ideas about the non-fiction texts they read.

GETTING READY

✔ Display the "Prompts to Grow Your Own Ideas" one-day chart (see Teaching).

✔ Prepare to read an excerpt from "The Battle Over GMOs" as you demonstrate how to grow ideas about the class research topic (see Teaching).

✔ Prepare to add a new bullet to the "How to Research a New Topic. . ." anchor chart (see Link).

✔ Print "Back Up Your Ideas," "Prompts to Grow Your Own Ideas," and "When a Text Contradicts Your Ideas, Ask . . ." mini-charts to support students (see Conferring and Small-Group Work).

MINILESSON

CONNECTION

Remind readers of the work they've done so far in this bend of the unit.

"Readers, at the start of this bend, you took on a new challenge, reading across many texts to learn more about a topic rather than just reading one larger text. To do this well, you must draw upon everything you've learned about how to read nonfiction well. You build your background knowledge on the topic early on. You study ways texts fit together and look more closely when they contradict each other. You do some research when things aren't making sense, and you work to understand the topic's lingo."

Share a quote about blindly following an authority, and compare this to the work readers do when they think only about what the author is teaching.

"You know Albert Einstein? He once said, 'Blind belief in authority is the greatest enemy of truth.' He's saying that if you follow someone just because they say they're in charge and knowledgeable, without questioning what they say, without talking back, without growing your own ideas, then you might not find out what the truth is. This got me thinking about another important thing to consider when you are reading nonfiction, especially when you've done as much work as you have to understand your texts. Nonfiction texts are written to teach information, but you still can't accept them blindly."

❖ **Name the teaching point.**

"Today I want to teach you that when you read nonfiction, you can't just accept the central ideas and facts authors teach you at face value. You also have to be reading to grow your own ideas about your texts, to develop your own theories about your topic."

TEACHING

Share prompts to help readers grow their own ideas about the text. Demonstrate how you read on in the text, and then pause to grow ideas about your topic, using the thought prompts to help you.

"When I'm growing ideas about texts or a topic, there are some prompts that help me." I displayed a short list. "Watch how I use these prompts to help me. I'm going to read a bit and then pause to grow ideas. Will you be ready to suggest a prompt I could use if I get stuck?

"Here's another part of 'The Battle Over GMOs.' I'm going to read it looking out for parts where I could grow my thinking." I started to read.

> Today, 94 percent of soybeans and 93 percent of corn planted in the U.S. is genetically altered—and most of it ends up in processed foods.
>
> According to the Grocery Manufacturers Association, up to 80 percent of what you eat has GMOs—but you might not know it. Unlike the European Union and places like India and Russia, the U.S. doesn't require foods with GMOs to be labeled.

"Huh . . . the U.S. doesn't require foods with GMOs to be labeled. Let me try growing some thinking about that. Okay, so *the text says* that the U.S. doesn't require foods with GMOs to be labeled, whereas the European Union, India, and Russia all do. *This makes me think* that the U.S. should have stricter laws about labeling, just like other countries, especially since only 37% of Americans think GMOs are safe."

I paused, gesturing for students to call out another prompt. One called out, "*This makes me wonder . . .*" I continued, "*This makes me wonder* why GMOs aren't labeled here. It kind of reminds me of the fast food industry and how we learned that they try not to pay workers as much money. I'm wondering if the GMO industry fights to keep GMOs unlabeled."

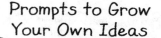

Prompts to Grow
Your Own Ideas

The text says...
This makes me think... °

A thought I have about this is...

My idea differs from the
author's when...

I think...

This makes me wonder...

One theory I'm growing is...
because...

Debrief, and restate the transferable work you just modeled.

"Did you see how I read a bit of text, this time on the lookout for places where I could grow my thinking? I took a fact that stood out to me, and I thought a lot about it, using prompts to help me. Lingering with one fact for a while helped me grow some deeper thinking."

ACTIVE ENGAGEMENT

Recruit students to try this with a text on their topic.

"Ready to try this with your research group? As a group, choose one text you can work with to grow ideas. Will one of you read a little bit of the text aloud like I did, and the rest of you be ready to signal when you're starting to grow ideas?" I moved from group to group as students chose texts and began reading aloud.

Once most groups were reading, I voiced over, "You don't have to read much to start growing ideas. Use the prompts to help you grow ideas."

While students talked, I moved from club to club coaching in:

- "Ground your ideas in the text. Tell the details that led you to that idea."
- "Talk a lot off of one prompt."
- "Tell whether you agree or disagree with the ideas your group mates are having."

LINK

Emphasize the importance of balance between growing ideas and considering what the text teaches.

"Of course, as you head off to read today, and whenever you're reading nonfiction, whether it's in this class or in social studies or when you're getting a new pet, growing ideas matters." I added the new work to our anchor chart. "However, growing ideas is insufficient if you're not *also* reading to determine what the text is teaching. As you head off today, try out this new work of growing ideas *and* try out some of the other work on our anchor chart. Off you go!"

ANCHOR CHART

To Research a New Topic . . .

- Preview texts to identify repeating subtopics.
- Build up a bit of background knowledge quickly.
  - Sequence your texts. Start with easier texts—even videos!
  - Teach others what you're learning.
- Create a brief summary of the text.
  - Ask, "What's the author's central idea?"
  - Determine main ideas that support the central idea.
  - Say back the central and main ideas in a short paragraph.
- Synthesize across texts.
  - Fit with?
  - Extends?
  - Contradicts?
- Turn to outside resources to clear up confusions.
- Become an expert on the topic's lingo.
- **Grow your own ideas about what you're reading.**

Grow your own ideas.

Supporting Students in Growing Ideas

AS THIS UNIT LAUNCHED, you taught students that the quality of a book-club conversation depended heavily on what participants brought to it, and that bringing a list of facts and regurgitating them was insufficient. Instead, you encouraged students to ask questions and grow ideas as they read and to bring those to their club conversations.

As you plan for your conferring and small-group work today, you might first take a few minutes to reflect on the book-club conversations you've listened to over the last few weeks. Do students state an idea and then only back it up with one piece of evidence? Do they stick with their initial ideas and hold them tightly, even as they read more about a topic? Do they reject texts and evidence that don't fit with their ideas? If so, look to the conferring and small-group work suggestions detailed below for ways you can support your readers in growing more nuanced and evidence-based ideas.

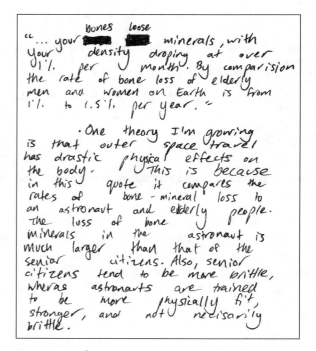

FIG. 14–1   Sofia writes to grow ideas about a key detail in the text.

If you see . . .	Then you can teach . . .	Leave students with . . .
A student grows an idea but can only point to one piece of evidence (or can only point to evidence from one text) to substantiate that idea.	"When you want to grow a particularly strong idea, it helps to make sure you can substantiate it, which means back it up with a lot of evidence. Specifically, it helps to ensure you have *multiple* pieces of evidence and that you can find evidence for your idea from *across* texts. If you can't find any additional evidence, sometimes that means you need to revise your initial idea to make it fit the available evidence." Ask the student to record an idea she is growing on a Post-it. "Will you take a few minutes to revisit your writing about reading and your texts with the idea you jotted down in mind? Look for additional pieces of evidence across texts that fit your idea. When you find one, flag it with a Post-it or jot it down. If you can't find any, or if you only find evidence in one text, you may need to revise your initial idea."	**Back Up Your Ideas:** • Multiple pieces of evidence from one text • Evidence from *across* texts
A student records an initial idea with evidence, but could push for deeper thinking about that idea.	"You're off to a strong start with growing ideas about your topic, but I think you can push yourself further. Just like your writing about reading, your ideas will be stronger if you consider a second or third idea, rather than just sticking with your first idea. "One way to do this is to write long about your idea. You can start by jotting down your idea. Then, you can choose a prompt and write a lot off of it. When you run out of things to say, choose another prompt and write a lot off of that one. Often, as you write, your idea starts to evolve and get more precise. "Ready to try it? Jot your idea, and then use these prompts to grow your thinking. Try to push yourself to a second or third idea."	**Prompts to Grow Your Own Ideas:** • "The text says . . . This makes me think . . ." • "A thought I have about this is . . ." • "My idea differs from the author's when . . ." • "I think . . ." • "This makes me wonder . . ." • "One theory I'm growing is . . . because . . ."
A student rejects a text because the author makes claims, includes facts, etc. that contradict his or her own ideas.	"I noticed that you put this text aside and decided not to read it because it said something you disagreed with. That's often our first impulse, to ignore if it contradicts our own ideas. "Instead of rejecting a text outright, you might let the text affect your thinking. To do that, you have to read the text carefully asking, 'What is this author's claim? What reasons does the author give to back up the claim? What evidence? Would you say the claim is substantiated, backed up by the evidence, or unsubstantiated?' "And, if the other author's points are well substantiated, you may consider rethinking your initial idea."	**When a Text Contradicts Your Ideas, Ask . . .** • What is this author's claim? • What reasons and evidence does the author give to back up the claim? • Is the claim substantiated or unsubstantiated? • How might this text lead me to rethink my ideas?

Talking Long to Develop Ideas

Set students up to meet in research groups to talk long to develop the ideas they started growing during today's workshop. Coach in as students develop their ideas through talk.

"Today, readers, you'll be meeting with your research groups during the share. Will you use this time to share some of the ideas you're already growing and see if you can make them even deeper? Partners, you can help with this work of idea-growing by asking your partner questions. If your partner says, 'I'm thinking that building the first atomic bomb was an incredibly bad idea,' you might ask, 'What makes you think that?' Or 'What would someone who disagrees say back to that?' Question each other in ways that help you to think more deeply about your ideas.

"Choose an idea you think you could grow even further, and get started talking."

SESSION 14 HOMEWORK

TIME IS DWINDLING: PRIORITIZING YOUR LAST-MINUTE RESEARCH

Readers, tomorrow is the last day of this bend. After that, we begin the final stretch of this unit, and you will be researching new topics. So think critically about the reading work you'll do tonight to solidify what you know about your topic. You might:

- Read texts on your topic you have not yet read and want to read.

- Reread some of the trickiest texts on your topic, now that you have built up more background knowledge.

- Read texts that help you further explore the new ideas you're growing.

Developing Carefully Curated Text Sets

Ɗear Teachers,

As the second bend draws to a close, we recommend you take a day to celebrate all your students have learned by giving them time to showcase their topics and learning. Soon, they will begin investigating a second topic, this time with more independence.

Years ago, when Donna Santman worked at the Teachers College Reading and Writing Project, she taught us about the importance of engaging students in the critical, yet challenging work of curating text sets on topics they know well. Kids would look across all the texts they had read on a topic, be it fiction or nonfiction, and then select the most powerful texts, the ones that introduced new perspectives or insights, and cobble them together into a recommended text set. Those curated text sets would get added to the classroom library and cherished by readers to come.

Today, then, you might invite students to leave their mark on their classroom and classmates by assembling a carefully curated selection of texts, which represents the must-read titles on their topic. These curated collections, consisting of four to six texts and a little write-up about why each text is in the collection, can be added to the classroom library and become starter reading material for students who select that topic as the one they will investigate and read about in Bend III. These text sets position their curators to act as experts, available to guide new kids who are interested in tackling the same topic.

To start, you might rally students to this new work by explaining curation. For instance, you could explain how an art curator pores over pieces, first to determine the best pieces for a gallery show and then to outline the most ideal wall arrangement. Or you could explain how music producers analyze the song list that could go on an album, and then make decisions about which songs should be included to advance a certain theme or tell a specific story.

Developing a text set starts with curation, and we recommend you give students some criteria to consider as they look across the texts they've read to determine which should be included in their final collection. You could walk students through a list that looks like the "When Curating a Text Set . . ." chart.

Then, you could share a sample of a curated text set. You'll find an example of one on genetic engineering in the online resources. You might show students how once you identified texts, you wrote up a brief, one- to two-paragraph description of each text, which included a brief summary and a rationale for why this text—out of all the texts on the topic—was included.

This work is complex, so you'll want to give students the majority of the period to work in their research groups to curate texts and create a written guide to their work. As they work, circulate the room and coach. Be on the lookout for students who are not drawing on their earlier learning about crafting a concise summary of a text, and coach them to identify a text's central idea(s) and key supportive details.

You'll want to leave time at the end of class for students to display their curated text sets. To make the work feel extra important, you might give each research group a new book bin or a special folder to decorate and add their texts to. Then, you'll want to celebrate all the new reading material that's being added to the library. You might point out that these collections now join the ranks of the likes of other bins in your library. Congratulate students on their newfound areas of expertise—and on their newly developed ability to curate collections of nonfiction.

To set the class up for reading in Bend III (and for later this year), you might end by inviting students to study their classmates' text sets and jot a list of new topics they'd like to explore moving forward. Collect these lists at the end of class so you can look across them and form students into new research groups before Session 16. You might note that the class will now become sources of information, themselves—that kids can ask questions or guidance of classmates whose topic they will study during the final bend. Of course, you'll also want to talk up the importance of reading nonfiction reading across the year, not just in this one unit. Tell kids that they can always pick up one of their classmates' collections to grow knowledge about a topic, even if they don't select that topic to research during the final bend.

Of course, you'll also want to talk up the fact that as students have become more knowledgeable about particular topics of study, they've also become more adept as readers and researchers of nonfiction, *in general*. Congratulate them on this and let them know that you look forward to watching them in action as more independent, confident researchers in the final stretch of the unit. In the next bend, you'll encourage and teach toward independence, so that students have the support they need to in fact assume this stance.

All the best,
Katie

When Curating a Text Set...

☑ *Limit yourself to 4–6 texts.*

☑ *Choose texts that cover your whole topic and address all key subtopics.*

☑ *Choose texts that extend or contradict information in one another.*

☑ *Sequence the texts. Which texts should a newbie to the topic read first? Next?*

☑ *Craft a brief summary of each text and a description of why it is included.*

Essentail Articles on Outer Space:

① The Apollo Space Program – This article is essentail because it discusses the overall history of space travel. More specifically, it discusses the early history/beginning of space travel.

② What are the Benefits of Space Exploration – This article is essentail because it discusses the numerous bennifits of space exploration. In order for a beginner to understand space travel, it is important for them to understand how it can help society.

FIG. 15–1 Sofia explains why the texts she's recommending are essential.

Researching a New Topic with More Independence While Helping Students to Read Critically

A Letter to Teachers

ear Teachers,

r. Brian Cambourne outlines seven essential conditions that must be in place for learning to occur. This bend especially targets one of Cambourne's conditions of learning: practice. In this bend, you invite students to practice familiar work, to have a go at it again, as they dive into a new text set. As Cambourne suggests, you'll boost students' learning by giving them an opportunity to study a new topic under slightly changed conditions: a new research group, a new context, and new texts with their own complexities.

As this bend launches, you'll channel students to work in research groups to study a new topic, one they identified from studying their classmates' curated text sets in Session 15. You'll need to decide whether your research groups are functioning well and you want them to remain together for another bend, or whether research groups could benefit from a change. If you decide to switch up the groups, draw on what you learned from Bends I and II about helping research groups quickly get up to speed. We recommend you continue to research genetic engineering during your minilessons.

Right away, you'll rally students to be in charge of their own learning, and you'll support transference by teaching them that to research well, they'll need to draw on all they know about nonfiction reading and research from Bends I and II. Unlike the other two bends, this bend kicks off with a typical minilesson instead of a read-aloud. You'll coach students as they review familiar charts to remember the steps researchers typically go through as they research a new topic, and then you'll coach students as they preview their texts, notice subtopics that recur, and then read easier texts to build up a bit of background knowledge. Make sure the text sets students curated as part of Session 15, plus the original texts you made available to kids, are part of these book bins. The repeated practice students get across this session, with more independence will help move students' new learning toward independent use.

The curated text sets you and the students provide on each topic are a great start, but to truly answer some of their research questions, students will benefit from engaging in online research. To support their work, you'll engage students in an inquiry into the challenges that readers face when researching and reading texts online, and you'll introduce them to some key strategies that online researchers draw on, such as orienting themselves to new Web pages to determine how they work. Then, you'll encourage them to pose their own research questions and investigate them online, synthesizing the new information they learn with the information they've already learned on their topic.

As you engage in this work, think about the access to technology that your students will have. Are your readers matched one-to-one with devices? Do you have access to a cart of laptops or tablets? If so, you might decide to extend the online work for an additional day. You could develop your own minilesson around one of the biggest challenges your students are facing online, such as evaluating whether or not links are worth following or synthesizing information across online texts, instead of just clicking forward to the next text. Even if access to technology is more difficult, I encourage you to think about ways to give your kids access to online research. If you can secure devices for each partnership or group, students can spend the period researching collaboratively. If you have only a few devices, you might set students up to rotate through the devices over the last few days of the unit. And, of course, remember that students can do Internet research on their smart phones!

Another way you'll lift the level of your students' work is by supporting critical reading. First, you'll coach students as they read and reread their texts to determine the author's point of view. You'll use a series of texts to make this point clear to your students, moving from advertisements and texts where an author's point of view is explicitly stated to texts where the author's point of view is embedded. Then, you'll extend that work, introducing them to a few common techniques authors use to advance their points of view, such as highlighting certain voices and leaving others out and including words that spark emotions. This read-aloud will equip students to think critically about why an author might have written a text.

Next, you'll extend this work by teaching students that when texts directly contradict one another, it helps to study the texts closely, asking, "Which is more trustworthy?" You'll introduce students to a test they can give a text to determine if it's trustworthy, asking questions such as, "Who wrote this text? What's their background?

When was this text written? Is it current?" Students will be able to answer some of their questions right in the text, and they might need to do some online research to determine answers to the others.

As students do this work, keep in mind another one of Cambourne's key conditions of learning: approximation. You want to see students giving this critical reading work a try, but it's likely they won't master this work in the span of two days. Whenever students are engaged in nonfiction reading across the year, coach them to consider the author's point of view and how it's advanced, as well as which text is most trustworthy.

To wrap up the unit, you'll invite students to give their own mini TED-style talks—short and engaging talks focused on the topics they researched across Bend III. They might plan a talk on one of the central ideas related to their topic or about something new and surprising that they learned while researching. Time spent planning for these talks is time spent away from reading, so you'll want to devote just one class period to students planning for their mini TED-style talks. Expect these talks to be rough drafts, not perfectly polished presentations, and for students to draw on their notes and what they've learned about nonfiction reading as they plan. Once students have planned for their talks, rally them to deliver their talks for audiences. You might take one student from each research group and gather them together, and then you could invite each student to deliver a TED-style talk to the rest of the group.

As this unit draws to a close, consider how you'll help your students sustain their nonfiction reading lives over the weeks to come. You might suggest that students weave nonfiction chapter books into their ongoing reading lives or that they listen to the TED-style talks thinking, "Which of these topics am I most interested in researching going forward?" Or, you might consider how students can draw on their learning in their science and social studies work, perhaps sharing anchor charts and key teaching points with your colleagues if your school is departmentalized.

Across this bend, pay particular attention to students' reading volume. If you do not have enough texts to keep kids reading about their topic for at least an hour a day, you might modify the homework. Instead of reading more about their topic, students could read nonfiction chapter books, other nonfiction trade books, or fiction texts. Do whatever you can to ensure students do a large volume of reading.

All the best,
Katie

Launching a New Round of Research Groups with Greater Independence

IN THIS SESSION

TODAY YOU'LL teach students that whenever researchers study a new topic, they draw on all they know about reading and research.

TODAY YOUR STUDENTS will begin researching a new topic by making a plan for how their research will go, which will involve getting the lay of the land of their topic and then reading easier resources to build up knowledge.

GETTING READY

✔ Before this session, you'll need to form new research groups that will stay together throughout this bend. Use students' lists of preferences that they generated at the end of Bend II to help you group them according to their topic interests. Be sure that each student has a partner within the group for activities that work best in pairs. Make a seating chart that you'll display at the beginning of this session to help students find the meeting space for their group.

✔ Display the "To Research a New Topic . . ." anchor chart to remind students of their learning from Bend II (see Teaching, Active Engagement, and Link).

✔ Provide each group with chart paper and markers to build a list of subtopics. Alternatively, students may build this list in their reader's notebooks (see Teaching and Active Engagement).

✔ Provide students with Post-its to jot their reading goals (see Share).

✔ Create a "Class Goals" chart for students to display their goals (see Share).

MINILESSON

CONNECTION

Introduce students to their new topic groups. Explain that since the amount of knowledge in the world is rapidly expanding, readers need to be able to research independently to keep learning.

"When you come to the meeting area, please note the new seating chart." I gave the students a minute to gather in their new spots, and then continued. "During our last reading workshop, you had a chance to study your classmates' curated text sets, and you thought about which topic you most wanted to study over the upcoming week. Last night, I grouped you based on the topics you were interested in, and now you are sitting next to your new research group, with a whole new bin of texts. I also partnered you up with someone in your research group, for times that it will be helpful to work in pairs. I know you're dying to start studying atomic bombs, climate change, and teen activism.

"I'm not sure that you realize this, but the amount of information in the world is expanding at a super-fast rate. Eric Schmidt, a leader at Google, said that every two days, there is as much new information produced as had been produced in the entire history of the world up until 2003. Isn't that incredible? If you want to keep learning, you can't sit back and wait for me to teach you something new each day. Listen up."

❖ **Name the teaching point.**

"Today I want to remind you that whenever you begin researching something new, you have to be in charge of your own learning. You have to draw on all you know about reading and research to make a plan for your new research project, and then put that plan into action."

TEACHING AND ACTIVE ENGAGEMENT

Rally students to develop a plan for their research. Coach them as they first revisit a familiar chart and remind themselves of steps readers go through when they research a new topic.

"Ready to be in charge? I'll coach you through some of the big steps, but you and your club will have to draw on all you know to make your work as strong as you can.

"Here goes. Whenever you're doing something new, it helps to remind yourself of what you already know about doing that kind of work. With your new group, read over our 'To Research a New Topic . . .' chart and remind yourselves of the steps you go through when you're researching a new topic. Name each step, and then talk about what that step means." I gave students a minute to talk.

Name what readers do first: preview repeating subtopics to get a sense of what the topic will cover. Set clubs up to do this as you coach in.

"I heard you saying that whenever you read nonfiction, you've got to start by previewing the texts. In this case, when you're reading across lots of texts, you've got to preview the texts to identify subtopics that repeat, so you know what the big things are that you'll learn about as you read. Ready to try this?

"Pull the texts out of your text set, and start poring over them, on the lookout for subtopics that repeat again and again. Figure out how you'll record those subtopics. You might make one chart for your group or each record them in your own notebooks."

ANCHOR CHART

To Research a New Topic . . .

- Preview texts to identify repeating subtopics.
- Build up a bit of background knowledge quickly.
  - Sequence your texts. Start with easier texts—even videos!
  - Teach others what you're learning.
- Create a brief summary of the text.
  - Ask, "What's the author's central idea?"
  - Determine main ideas that support the central idea.
  - Say back the central and main ideas in a short paragraph.
- Synthesize across texts.
  - Fit with?
  - Extends?
  - Contradicts?
- Turn to outside resources to clear up confusions.
- Become an expert on the topic's lingo.
- **Grow your own ideas about what you're reading.**

Grow your own ideas.

This makes me think.... The text says. This makes me wonder.

I gave students three or four minutes to begin previewing their texts and generating subtopics while I coached in:

- "Look for subtopics that repeat."

- "Repeating subtopics won't always show up with the same words. Look out for synonyms."

- "That list of subtopics is getting long. Look across them and see if you can fit any together."

Remind students that readers sequence texts from easiest to hardest and read the easiest texts on their topic first to build up some background knowledge. Coach them as they sequence their texts.

"Now you've got a starter list of subtopics. Let's keep going. You mentioned that next, readers build up a bit of background knowledge by sequencing their texts from easiest to hardest, and then reading the easiest texts first so they can learn some of the important words and concepts related to their topic. Try this out. Lay out your texts as a group, and look for the easiest ones to read first."

As students worked, I voiced over with tips:

- "You might need to read a few lines to get a sense of whether a text is easy or hard."

- "Easier texts aren't always shorter. Look for texts that give an overview of the topic. Those are often easier."

- "You might glance at the texts' layouts to see which texts have more supportive structures. Look for clear chapter titles and bold headings that give clues about the content. These might be good texts to start with."

Don't pause your lesson to wait until each group has completed each step. Instead, give students a few minutes to try the work before moving on. Students can always come back to finish this work during independent reading time. The fact that they have started it here, with you, will make them more likely to continue the work on their own.

LINK

Encourage research groups to generate a plan for the work they will do, and then send them off to start researching.

"Readers, I could keep coaching you through each of these steps, but I think you're ready to continue researching on your own. As you do, remember to draw on all you know to help you read and research.

"With your group, make a plan for how your research will go as you investigate your new topic. Think about whether you'd rather read easier texts on your own or with your partner. Plan for when you'll stop and teach each other about the basics you're learning. Will you stop along the way to talk or wait until the end of reading? And, whatever plan you make, keep in mind all you know about note-taking. Remember to synthesize information as you take notes and to keep your note-taking brief. When you have a plan, head off to get started!"

Rallying Students to the Work of the New Bend

TODAY, you invited students to study a new research topic in groups with more independence, drawing on all they learned in Bends I and II about reading nonfiction well and researching well. Expect to see students approximate much of their earlier learning. For instance, you'll want to see that students start with easier, overview texts before reading the more challenging texts on their topic. You'll want to look for evidence that students are setting up files in their notebook and sorting the new information they're learning into those files. And, you'll want to see students considering central ideas as they read.

I recommend you coach students with a light touch today. After all, one of your major goals is to support research groups in working independently. If your support is too heavy-handed, you won't provide students the opportunity to move toward greater independence and to practice solving problems on their own. Rather than watching with eagle eyes for ways your students are messing up and need coaching, you might watch for ways they are just on the brink of mastering new work and celebrate that. Naming what kids are doing well is always a great way to get more of something going.

Of course, many students will need deeper instruction than pointed compliments will provide. After spending a few minutes observing, you might do some quick check-ins with research groups. Make your feedback focused and direct. Act flabbergasted when students aren't doing something you taught them to do. Then, quickly empower them to solve their problems in ways that support transferable skills and independence. Make notes to support these students in the coming days with more in-depth conferences and small groups.

Use the following chart to guide your observations and tips.

If you see . . .	Then you could say . . .
Students' choice of texts seems almost random.	"I noticed you each jumped in and chose a text quickly. Will you look over our charts from earlier in this unit? There are things you can do that will really help you research that you aren't doing yet. Once you find some, try them out with your club. Get started!"
Students are note-taking, but they're not drawing on what they learned in Bends I and II.	"I'm noticing that the notes you took today look really different than the notes you took earlier in the unit. That's surprising to me, because at this point, you know how to take notes that are way stronger than the notes you're taking today. Once you know how to do better, you should be doing better whenever you read and jot! "Will you take a few minutes to remind yourselves of what you did earlier in this unit as you were note-taking? Look back at your notes to help spark your memory. Once you have some ideas in mind, make a plan for how you can make your notes even stronger."

If you see . . .	Then you could say . . .
Students are stuck and appealing to you for help.	"I can tell you're really working hard to understand what you're reading, and you're paying attention to when things don't make sense. Here's the thing, though. Most of the time, I won't be here with you when you need to solve a problem. Instead, you'll have to figure out how to solve your problems on your own. "To do this, you could study the charts up in our room to see if any of them hold answers. Maybe you need a review on what to do when you encounter tricky words. Or maybe you need a refresher on identifying subtopics. You could generate a few possible solutions to your problems. You could say, 'Maybe . . .' and name out one possibility, and then 'Could it be . . .' or 'Perhaps . . .' Name out a few possible solutions until you find one that might work, and then try it out. I'll admire you as you brainstorm together."
New research groups are having difficulties working together.	"It seems like your group is having a little trouble adjusting to one another. Can I share a tip with you that might help your group get up and running quickly? You might start by establishing a few norms. You could decide as a club what you need to work together well, based on what worked well in your earlier book clubs and research groups. These might be things like taking turns for who gets to talk first, or establishing temporary roles like facilitator to get things going. Once you've got a little list of norms you can all agree to, then you can get started working on your reading again with those norms in mind. Are you up for trying that? Great! Get started."

Tracking Progress toward Goals

Channel students to check in on the goals they set earlier in the unit and to determine whether they need to continue working on those goals or set new goals. Coach in as they work.

"Readers, instead of meeting with your research group today, will you use our share time to do some reflecting? Right before you started researching your first topic, you set a goal, and you've been working on that goal for about a week and a half now. When you're working toward something, it helps to stop and monitor your progress along the way.

"Right now, will you pull out the goal you've been working on? Check in with yourself around that goal. Have you been working on that goal regularly? You might flip through your notebook or study your Post-its. Can you point to evidence of where you've worked on that goal?" I gave students a minute or two to reflect.

"If you haven't met a goal yet, you'll probably want to make a plan to keep working on it. But, if you've met a goal already, will you think about what new goals you'll work toward? Use our anchor charts to help you. Whatever you decide, jot your goals down."

As students worked, I circulated. I voiced over goals students set to give other students an example of how their goals could go. "Oh, synthesizing information across texts is a big goal. Yes, growing your own ideas early on is definitely important."

Ask students to post their goals publicly before leaving the room.

"Before you head off, will you jot the goals you set on a Post-it note with your name on it and stick it up on our 'Class Goals' chart? Posting your goals publicly can help hold you accountable to your goal and can help you find other kids who are working on that same goal."

Build Up Background Knowledge

 Plan

A plan that I could follow would be to...

° Notice the big ideas about the topic and learn a little bit about what they are and why they matter

° Think about what you know about the topic (even if it isn't super specific) and do a little bit of thinking about what that might mean

° Find some more general information about the topic oppose to specific dates and facts.

FIG. 16–1   Paige develops a plan to build up background knowledge on her new topic.

WORKING TOWARD GOALS WHILE RESEARCHING A NEW TOPIC

Tonight, continue exploring your new research topic. Aim for about forty minutes of reading. As you do, remember to draw on all you've learned as readers to help you read these new nonfiction texts well. Will you especially work on the goals you set today? Do you need to read more to meet that goal? Think across more texts? Read alert to something in particular? Jot a few notes. Do what you need to do to make progress toward that goal.

As you read tonight, think about some big questions you have on your topic that you'd like to research further. Will you jot down two or three questions? Having a few research questions in mind will help you research in more powerful ways.

Inquiry into the Particular Challenges of Online Research

GETTING READY

✔ Develop a research question to investigate, and choose a website that will allow you to research that question. We chose the research question, "What is GMO labeling like outside of the United States?" and the Just Label It! website. A link to this website is available in the online resources. Be prepared to project the website you selected (see Teaching and Active Engagement).

✔ Be sure students have their reading notebooks with them in the meeting area (see Teaching and Active Engagement).

✔ Have chart paper and markers available to provide a note-taking model and to create a class chart (see Teaching and Active Engagement).

✔ Ensure students have access to a digital device (computers, tablets, smart phones) for conducting online research. Students can work in partnerships, if needed (see Link).

✔ Have your own device (computer, tablet, smart phone) available for quick demonstrations of strategies for online research (see Conferring and Small-Group Work).

✔ Provide chart paper to research groups to generate lists of problems and solutions (see Share).

IN THIS SESSION

TODAY YOU'LL engage students in an inquiry into the challenges readers face when researching and reading texts online.

TODAY YOUR STUDENTS will research their topics online, and as they read, they'll record the challenges they encounter and develop solutions to tackle those challenges.

MINILESSON

CONNECTION

Call to mind the questions students developed for homework, and share an example to demonstrate a challenge they may encounter when researching their questions.

"Readers, last night for homework, you thought about some big questions you have on your topics that you'd like to research further. I'm wondering if some of you are having the same experience when you research that I'm having. I start with questions about a topic, or I let the texts I'm reading spark questions for me, and I read on with those questions in mind.

"But here's the thing. Often, the texts I'm reading don't come straight out and answer my questions. So, I'm inspired to conduct further research. As with most of us these days, my first thought is, 'I'll google it.'

"Let me give you an example. Last night, I came across an article about whether GMOs should be labeled. As I was reading all about the reasons for and against labeling, I picked up on a few hints about labeling in other countries. I couldn't help but wonder how GMO labeling is handled outside of the United States. I could see the text wasn't going to answer my question directly, so, naturally, I headed to Google. I typed in 'What is GMO labeling like outside of the United States?' and of course, I got a ton of results. Over 34 million, to be exact.

"This got me thinking about how most of the research we do these days is online, but online research has its own set of challenges. Are you up for studying some of these challenges alongside me today?"

Name the inquiry question.

"Today, let's adopt a problem-solving mind-set. Let's investigate the following questions. 'What are the biggest challenges that we face when researching online? How do we solve those challenges?'"

TEACHING AND ACTIVE ENGAGEMENT

Set students up to research you as you work with a website. Ask them to jot down the challenges you encounter and ways you solve those challenges.

"To investigate this, I thought you could research me as I conduct some online research. I'll probably encounter a bunch of challenges, and I'll do my best to solve them. Will you jot down the challenges you notice I encounter, as well as any ways you see me try to solve those challenges? Later, we can compile your notes so you've got a tool to use whenever you encounter these challenges in your online research.

"It might help to set up your notes as a T-chart, with one column for jotting challenges I face and another for ways you see me solve those challenges. Of course, you could decide to set up your notes differently."

Challenges Faced	Possible Solutions
#1:	
#2:	
#3:	
#4:	

Although you could distribute a pre-made note-taking template, it's important work for students to create their own note-taking system. This work will just take students thirty seconds or so, but it will prepare them to create their own note-taking systems as needed in the future.

Demonstrate how you orient yourself to a website, asking, "Who is it set up for? When does the text get to the information I'm looking for?"

I pulled up the Google search results. "Ready to start researching me? Remember the question I searched, 'What is GMO labeling like outside of the United States?' I think I'll start on the first hit in my search results, which is a link from the Just Label It! website." I clicked on the link. "Let me pause for a minute to orient myself to this text. It helps to think,

'Who is the text set up for? And, when does the text get to the information I'm looking for?' I hope you're watching me closely, researchers, and jotting notes about what you notice. Oh, it gets to the information I want right away." I read aloud from the page, "'Currently, 64 countries around the world require labeling of genetically modified foods. Unlike most other developed countries—such as 28 nations in the European Union, Japan, Australia, Brazil, Russia, and even China—the U.S. has no laws requiring labeling of genetically modified foods.' Then, I see a list of all of the countries that require labeling. But when I try to click on one of the countries for more information, I see they aren't clickable." I clicked on the countries a bunch of times to show how clicking didn't take me anywhere.

"I see a lot of links to other pages about labeling, so this site could have some more useful information. I'll visit the home page to see if I can find out more about this website. I'll click the logo at the top left, since the logo usually links you to the homepage. Whoa! There's a ton of stuff on this page: pictures, text boxes, ad campaigns, links to Facebook and Twitter, even recent blog posts.

"Okay, let's see. I know that many websites are written for a particular audience or are angled in a particular way. I'm going to scan the text thinking, 'Who is this text set up for?' I think it's set up for people who want all GMOs to be labeled, because I see scrolling titles like 'Consumers Want to Know Which Ingredients Are Genetically Modified' and headings about how Hershey's and Nestlé should label whether there are GMOs in their foods. As I scroll down, I see a bunch of blog posts with titles like 'Expert Panel Confirms Importance of GMO Labeling.' So, it looks like the text is mostly set up for people who want to label GMOs. I don't see anything about what labeling is actually like in other countries."

Demonstrate how you return to the search results and continue researching if your first attempt was not successful. Point out how you orient yourself each time you arrive at a new Web page.

"That link didn't really give me the detailed information I was looking for, so I think I'll try another link. I see the next link in my search results is from the same website, so I'll skip that one. I'll try the third link, from the Council for Foreign Relations." I clicked on it. "I'll start by orienting myself to the text again. I see it's an article based on a case study that looks really dense and confusing-looking. Maybe it's written for scientists or lawmakers. I see links to a bunch of different articles, but it doesn't look like any of them are about GMOs. Oh, and look at this, it's dated 2001. That's a long time ago. I think the information will be too outdated to be helpful."

Channel students to share some of the challenges they've noticed, then demonstrate one final search.

"Right now, would you turn to your partner and tell each other a couple of challenges you've already noticed?"

I gave students a moment to talk, and then I continued, "Many of you are noticing issues such as how hard it can be to find specific information, and how often really confusing or dense texts come up in search results. Let's try one more link, and then we'll record some of the challenges you're noticing.

"Rather than just click the next link, I think I'll scan the search results to try to find a more promising website." I scanned the results, and then said, "Most of these links are about GMO labeling in the U.S. I don't think any of them will help

Websites are constantly evolving documents. This information was current as of the publication date of this unit, but it will regularly change. You'll want to study the current content of the website you select and design a similar inquiry. Notice what is highlighted within this demonstration and pop those things out as you demonstrate. The bold print across the lesson will be a particularly helpful resource.

me answer my question. I'm going to have to refine my search question. I'll try to find out how labeling is handled in specific places."

I typed in *GMO labeling in Europe*. "I'll click on this link, and I'll quickly orient myself. On the right of the page, it says this site is from the Food Standards Agency for the United Kingdom. There's a lot of dense text on this page, but I see that it has bolded subtitles that can help me to navigate the text. I see 'Will the label tell me if food is GM?' 'Examples of labeling requirements,' and 'Short consultation: EU harmonisation of "GM-free" labelling.' Great, I'll jump to the section about labels for food to try and find my answer. Let's see. Oh, it says, 'In the EU, if a food contains or consists of genetically modified organisms (GMOs), or contains ingredients produced from GMOs, this must be indicated on the label. For GM products sold "loose," information must be displayed immediately next to the food to indicate that it is GM.'

"Finally, I have an answer to my question, or at least I know how labeling is handled in Europe."

Channel research groups to compare the lists of challenges and possible solutions they jotted down. Develop a class chart of challenges and possible solutions.

"Readers, gather in your research groups, and compare your lists of challenges and possible solutions. I'll listen and jot some notes so we can develop a class chart." I listened in while students talked and charted some of what I overheard.

"All right readers, turn back. I captured some of what I heard you saying."

Time is of the essence whenever you teach through inquiry. If you have students share out their responses with the whole class, your lesson will easily run long. Instead, listen in as students are talking in research groups and jot a few of their responses. You could always say, "I heard you saying . . ." and then quickly jot what students said after you send them off to read.

Challenges Faced	Possible Solutions
#1: Each website is set up differently.	• Preview each text, asking, "Who is it set up for? When does the text get to the information I'm looking for?"
#2: It's hard to figure out how the site works physically.	• Investigate what clicks and what doesn't.
#3: The text is challenging or confusing.	• Skim for the information you need (headings, text features).
#4: The text doesn't answer a research question.	• Try a new, more specific search.

LINK

Emphasize that as students research online, they need to adopt a problem-solving mind-set. Encourage them to read and research online today and to record challenges and solutions.

"You identified a bunch of challenges readers encounter when researching online, as well as possible solutions. But this is just the beginning. There won't be time here for us to solve every problem you might face. Instead, it matters that you develop a problem-solving mind-set. I got out a bunch of different devices: some computers, some iPads, some of you will even use cell phones. Will you use some of your reading time today to research online? Use the research questions you generated last night for homework, as well as any new ones you develop as you're researching today to guide your research.

"As you research today, be on the lookout for problems you face, embrace those problems, and then get started trying to tackle them. If you encounter new problems or solutions, jot them down so that you can add them to our class conversation about this later. Remember, also, that you're still learning about your topic as you research, so you should definitely do a little jotting about what you learn from the texts you study."

Challenges faced	Possible solutions
Vocabulary level	Writing for kids or for begginers.
	Use dictionary
Sources -not reliable	Trying to find a source on a book
not specific results	You can put quotes over your question toset more spefic results.
	Adding more spefic information in your question.

FIG. 17–1   Mohamad jots challenges and possible solutions as he researches online.

Supporting Predictable Problems with Online Research

ONLINE RESEARCH MIGHT FEEL AUTOMATIC. You type in a search term, hit enter, and then click one of the search results. The truth is, though, that online researchers have to make a plethora of minuscule but important decisions whenever they research online. Pause for a moment and try researching with a hyper-awareness, noticing the small decisions that go into your research. What choices do you make? What strategies do you draw on? Perhaps when you get a list of search results, you begin by scanning all the search results on the first page, considering which search result will most likely yield the information you're looking for. Note these strategies so you can share them with your students.

There are a few predictable problems your students are likely to encounter as they begin researching online. These problems are detailed below, along with possible language you can use during conferences to teach key strategies. If you have your own device—a computer, tablet, or cell phone—you might carry that device with you as you confer. That way, if you find students who would benefit from a quick demonstration, you'll be able to model how you use a strategy online.

Students are reading a text that is too difficult.

Even with the bells and whistles of online research, keep in mind that your big work is to help students become better *readers*. One of the major challenges with reading online is that the vast majority of texts students encounter are quite difficult. Websites are filled with unfamiliar information, complex vocabulary, and long, unwieldy sentences. Students can learn to navigate them with support, and to do so it is crucial that they draw upon all they have learned about effective nonfiction reading as they work. If you pull up next to a student reading a challenging text, there are a few things you could say that might help.

- **Search for easier texts on the same topic:** "These texts are super-challenging. Something that helps me is to look for much easier texts on the topic I'm researching. I'll type in my search terms, and then I'll add 'for kids'

or 'easy version' or 'simple explanation' into the search bar, and then hit enter. Usually, some of the results that pop up are easier to read than the results I encountered before."

- **Skim to find the parts you need to read:** "When you really want to read a tough site, it helps to start by skimming to find the information you need. That way, you can zoom in on just the parts of the text that you really need to read and read those carefully, with your mind on high."

- **Chunk and summarize the text:** "Whenever you're reading something difficult, whether it's an online text or a print text, there are a few simple strategies that can help. First, it helps to break texts into smaller chunks, and then to pause after those chunks to figure out the gist of what you just read. Sometimes, rereading particularly tricky chunks helps. It also helps to read with a partner, to tap a friend and say, 'Hey, this text is super-difficult. Can we read it together?'"

- **Read outside the text:** "Remember to draw on the strategies you know about reading difficult texts. When you encounter something unfamiliar, you can read outside the text to build up a big chunk of knowledge, and then reread the text with that new knowledge in mind."

Students are having trouble generating focused research searches.

One predictable problem while researching online is that students' searches are too open-ended. A student researching about diseases and illnesses might type in "diseases and illnesses" and then feel frustrated that the search results don't yield any particularly useful results. One easy tip is to suggest that students research their topic *and* a focused subtopic. For instance, students could type in "diseases and illnesses in the Middle Ages" or "diseases and illnesses and how to prevent them in children." Simply adding in a subtopic, in addition to the main topic, will yield more focused search results.

Students are quickly skimming sites but not reading anything in depth.

You might notice students who click on a search result, spend a minute scrolling up and down the page, and then move on to the next site. While skimming is helpful when trying to determine whether a site might yield useful information, skimming is not really reading.

If you notice students who are only skimming and scanning, you might say, "I'm noticing that you're only spending thirty seconds or a minute on a page before you jump to the next one. That kind of skimming and scanning won't yield the rich information you're looking for. Instead, as you skim, you want to be on the lookout for pages and sites you can read more closely. It helps to ask, 'What here interests me? What might yield useful information?' Then, when you find a page where a closer read will pay off, you can stop skimming and start reading."

Students are clicking on every link they encounter.

Some students might click on every link they encounter, even clicking on a link in the middle of a sentence before they finish reading all the way through that sentence. If this is the case, you might teach students that when readers encounter a link, they have to quickly evaluate the link to determine whether it's worth following. You might say, "Your Web page is filled with a ton of links—links to other pages and sites that are included in the middle of sentences. Right now, you're clicking on almost every link. Here's the thing, though. Some of those links will yield super-useful information, but many of them won't. When you encounter a link, it pays to predict what information that link *could* give you, and then to make a decision about whether the link is worth following, based on your prediction." You might give a brief demonstration of this, showing students how you think aloud about what a link might lead to. Then, coach students as they try this out on their own texts.

Also, readers who click on links rarely make it back to the original page to determine how the new information they are learning fits with the original information. This cross-text synthesis work is critical, so you'll want to address this right away. You might say, "Let me give you a tip. Right now, you're clicking from one page directly to the next, following the links. You're only thinking forward, about what's next. What will yield more useful thinking is that if you read a page, click on a link that's part of the text, and then return back to that original page. That way, you can consider how the new information fits with, extends, or contradicts what you originally read." Coach students as they try this work, following a link and then returning to the original text to see how the new information fits.

Exhibiting Challenges of Online Research

Channel students to gather in research groups to share the problems they encountered while reading. Ask them to chart each problem and then collaborate to list possible solutions.

"Readers, I've been watching you research online for the last thirty minutes. You've come across several new challenges. The thing is, since you're each studying different sites, you're encountering different challenges. So, I thought that to end today, it would help if you gathered together in your research groups to create a giant list of challenges people might encounter when reading websites and note some possible solutions. You'll probably be able to generate additional solutions to problems as you work together. Get started charting!"

Ask students to do a quick gallery walk of the problem-and-solution charts that other groups created, noting solutions other groups generated that they can try out later.

"You've got to take a look at all the charts your classmates have created. To wrap up our workshop today, let's do a quick gallery walk. Set up your chart almost like you'd set up an exhibit in a museum. I'll put on some background music. Will you wander from exhibit to exhibit, studying each chart and noting the challenges and the solutions that group generated? Take note of a solution that you'd like to try out the next time you encounter trouble."

READING AND RESEARCHING ONLINE AND THROUGH PRINT TEXTS

Tonight, continue your research about your topics. Aim to read and research for at least forty minutes. You can research online or read from print texts. Make sure you spend the bulk of your time reading, and not just searching and skimming for interesting information. Draw on all you know about tackling the challenges of nonfiction reading and online research. Spend four or five minutes of your reading time jotting notes on what you are learning. Consider whether the new information you are learning fits with, contradicts, or extends what you've already recorded in your notes to decide how and where you'll record the information.

Read-Aloud

*Determining the Author's Point of
View and How Its Advanced*

IN THIS SESSION

TODAY YOU'LL teach students that readers critically analyze an author's point of view, reading and rereading to determine the author's point of view, and noting a few techniques the author has used to convey it.

TODAY YOUR STUDENTS will reread an article with a particular focus on the author's point of view, and they will follow that by reading a new article on their topic.

CONNECTION

Set students up to check in about their reading volume and stamina.

"We're going to devote most of today to a read-aloud, and I have a lot to teach you about reading nonfiction—but all that teaching will be for naught if you aren't actually making time to read, and to read a lot outside of school. So before we do anything else, will you and your partner discuss the reading you're currently doing outside of school. How long are you reading for each night? How much are you reading in that time? How could you read more? Partners, your job is not just to listen. Your job is to be an advocate for reading in your partner's life. Try to find out what gets in the way of your partner doing more reading, and be a force for the good."

I gave students a few minutes to talk, circulating around the meeting area to note which students seemed to be on track with their reading volume and which students I needed to follow up with later.

CONDUCTING THE READ-ALOUD

Set up today's work by sharing a definition of author's point of view. Then, channel students to study an ad, noting some of the techniques the author uses to communicate his point of view.

"This is what you need to know before we get started on today's read-aloud. Every text you encounter—from a rap to a political advertisement to an article in the *New York Times*—is written by a person who has a particular point of view on the topic. Sometimes the author's point of view will be incredibly clear, like in this ad." I projected an ad from the World Wildlife Fund. "Will you study it with your partner? Think about what this author's point of view is, and note some of the techniques he's using to get his point of view across." I channeled students to turn and talk.

Name out the techniques you heard students mention. Then distribute a sheet that lists those techniques as well as a few more, and channel students to study the techniques with a partner.

"The techniques I heard you naming here are some of the common techniques authors use to get their point of view across to readers. You said the author states an opinion *directly*, that people should 'stop wildlife crimes.' And you said the author chose to include these two photos deliberately. One of you even called it 'shocking.' You also pointed out that this author includes words that spark emotions. *Ugly* has a pretty emotional charge. Authors use those techniques all the time to get their point of view across."

I displayed a large set of technique cards on the right-hand side of the board and distributed a smaller set to students. "There are a few other techniques authors often use. Will you and your partner study them? Then, choose one technique and talk about what it means." I gave students just a minute to talk, knowing I could highlight some of the trickiest techniques during the read-aloud.

Courtesy World Wildlife Fund

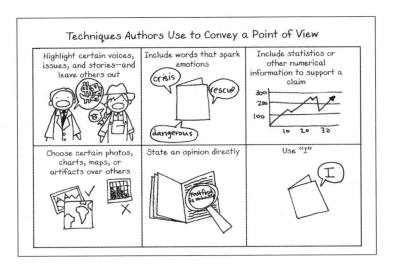

Read sections of the text aloud, and model how you study sections next to the technique cards, noting how the author's point of view is being conveyed in those sections.

Keep this example brief, so that you can spend your time on the trickier work.

"In articles, an author's point of view can still be pretty obvious." I displayed an article titled "Labels for GMO Foods Are a Bad Idea" and read aloud the title. "Do you see how the author of this article just comes out and states an opinion directly? The informational texts you're reading now usually won't work that way, so I chose a new text for us to study that I think is more similar to what you'll read. It's titled 'Scientists Make a Better Potato.' As I read it aloud, let's think critically about the author's point of view, because the author's point of view will often influence how the text is written." I started reading aloud.

Scientists Make a Better Potato

By Keith Ridler January 21, 2016

A potato genetically engineered to resist the pathogen that caused the Irish potato famine is as safe as any other potato on the market, the U.S. Food and Drug Administration says.

"Hmm, . . . I could keep powering through here, but I know authors often hint at their point of view early on in an article. Let me reread it to see if Keith Ridler uses any of those techniques to get his point of view across." I reread the lead. "Maybe he's including words that spark emotions. When he uses the word *better*, it seems like he wants us to feel good about these potatoes." I moved the "Include words that spark emotion" technique card to the left-hand side of the board.

Physically manipulating the cards that represent techniques authors use to convey their point of view helps draw particular attention to the techniques used in the article. It also gives students a model for how they can use the cards in their research groups.

"Let's read on. Be on the lookout for techniques the author is using—really obvious ones, like stating an opinion, and less obvious ones, like choosing particular people to quote." I continued reading.

The potato famine struck Ireland between 1845 and 1852, and about a million people died.

In a letter to Idaho-based J.R. Simplot Co., the FDA said the potato isn't substantially different in composition or safety from other products already on the market. It doesn't raise any issues that would require the agency to do more stringent premarket vetting.

"We're pleased and hope that consumers recognize the benefits once it's introduced into the marketplace next year," Doug Cole, the company's director of marketing and communications, said.

"Well, it doesn't seem like Keith Ridler is using any of the super-obvious techniques here, like stating an opinion directly or using *I*. Is he using any of the other techniques? I see the words *pleased*, *hope*, and *benefits*, and those seem like words that spark emotions. Oh, but wait a second, those words are inside a quote. That's what Doug Cole said, not what Keith Ridler thought.

"What about this one?" I said, picking up the technique card that read "Highlight certain voices, issues, and stories—and leave others out." "So far, it seems like the voices being heard are from places like the Food and Drug Administration. Remember how we read before that they approve GMOs for sale and don't require them to be labeled? And we're hearing from Doug Cole, but he's in charge of marketing for the company, which makes me think he wants to paint the potato in a good light. We're not hearing from anyone who is opposed to GMO products.

"So, it seems like another technique the author is using is that he *highlights certain voices, issues, and stories—and leaves others out*." I moved that technique to the left-hand side of the board.

Set students up to consider what techniques the author is using to communicate his point of view. Have students first summarize what happened and then name the author's techniques.

"Ready to try it? I'll read a little bit more aloud. Listen first to get the gist, and then we'll reread it to determine more techniques Keith Ridler uses to get his point of view across."

Before the potato is marketed to consumers, it must be cleared by the U.S. Environmental Protection Agency, Cole said. That's expected to happen in December.

The U.S. Department of Agriculture approved the potato in August.

The Russet Burbank Generation 2 is the second generation of Simplot's "Innate" brand potatoes. It includes the first version's reduced bruising. But it has less of a chemical produced at high temperatures that some studies have shown can cause cancer.

The second-generation potato also includes an additional trait. The company says it will allow potatoes to be stored at colder temperatures longer to reduce food waste.

Haven Baker, vice president of plant sciences at Simplot, said late blight remains the No. 1 pathogen for potatoes around the world. It was the cause of the Irish potato famine.

"This will bring 24-hour protection to farmers' fields and, in addition, has the potential to reduce pesticide spray by 25 to 45 percent," Baker said.

"Did you get the gist? Turn and summarize this part with your partner." I gave students thirty seconds to summarize, and then said, "I'll reread this part. Will you be on the lookout for what techniques Ridler is using to get his point of view across? He might be using the techniques he used earlier or new ones."

After I reread the section, I channeled students to turn and share what techniques they noticed Ridler using in the article.

Coach students as they brainstorm other people or groups who could have been quoted in the text and consider why the author would have included certain quotes instead of others.

"I heard you saying maybe this author *includes statistics or other numerical information to support a claim*." I moved that technique card to the left-hand side of the board. "One partnership said that Ridler includes a quote with statistics like, '24-hour protection,' and 'reduce pesticide spray by 25 to 45 percent.' These statistics may show Ridler's support of the genetically modified potato. Ridler didn't include statistics that show negative effects from the potato, such as results from insect studies.

"Others of you noticed that again, Ridler *highlights certain voices, issues, and stories and leaves others out*. He chose to quote the vice president of the potato company, the one that actually grew the potatoes, when he could have quoted someone different. Will you brainstorm some other groups of people Ridler could have quoted here, and consider why he chose someone from the potato company to quote?"

I moved from partnership to partnership as they talked, posing questions:

- "Brainstorm all the players. Who have we read about in other articles who is not quoted here?"
- "Why do you think the author chose that person over *all* the people he could have quoted?"
- "Whose voices are not heard in this article?"

I briefly summarized students' points. "I heard you saying that Ridler could have quoted a lot of different people: a farmer who grows GMOs, a scientist, a person who wants GMOs to be labeled, a person who refuses to eat genetically engineered foods. And you said maybe he chose the vice president of the plant because he's trying to show that the potatoes are a great thing."

Continue reading through the end of the text, and then channel students to name the techniques the author uses to get his point of view across.

"There's just a bit of the article left. Let's power through, considering which techniques Keith Ridler uses to get across his point of view. Get ready to summarize this part with your partner."

The late blight resistance comes from an Argentinian variety of potato that naturally produced a defense.

"There are 4,000 species of potatoes," Baker said. "There is an immense library to help us improve this great food. By introducing these potato genes, we can bring sustainability and consumer benefits."

The company has already been selling its first generation of Innate potatoes to consumers. Its 2014 crop was sold out and the company is selling the 2015 crop of about 2,000 acres.

Cole said those potatoes were mostly grown in Idaho and Wisconsin. They are being sold in supermarkets across the nation.

But one of the company's oldest business partners, McDonald's, has rejected using any of Simplot's genetically engineered potatoes.

Cole said the company plans to introduce the potatoes to other restaurants and hotel convention centers as precut and pre-peeled potatoes, where he said the resistance to bruising makes them a good product.

I read aloud the section, and I asked students to summarize what that part of the text taught with a partner. "Now, I'll display this part. Go back and study it with your partner, asking, 'What techniques does this author use to get his point of view across?' Remember he might be using more than one technique."

While partnerships talked, I coached in:

- "Don't just name the technique. Tell where you see evidence of that technique being used."

- "You found one technique this author used. Reread and see if he's using any other techniques here."

- "Brainstorm why the author might have used that technique. What ideas does that give you about his point of view?"

I moved the cards for the techniques students mentioned to the left-hand column of the chart.

Remind students of the techniques the author used. Rally students to consider what the author's point of view might be, based on how he's using the different techniques to convey his point of view.

"Okay, we've read this article and considered what techniques Keith Ridler is using to get across his point of view. Now, we have to figure out what his point of view might be. Let's look across what we've noticed so far. Hmm, . . . he uses words like *better* and *safe* to describe the potatoes. He's mostly including the story of the potato company and all the good potatoes can do, and he's mostly leaving out the stories of people who think the potatoes won't be safe to eat. He includes statistics that show benefits of the potatoes, not potential harm. He only mentions McDonald's not using the potatoes in one sentence, and he doesn't explain why. And, he's choosing to quote the potato company instead of other people. With your partner, see if you can figure out what Ridler's point of view might be about this topic."

Use the coaching tips that fill these lessons flexibly. If you think all students could use the tips, you might voice over to the class as students talk, raising the volume of your voice so students tune in. You might use the tips as you coach into partnerships, pausing their talk to share a tip that lifts the level of their work. Or, you could whisper one of these prompts into a student's ear, lifting the level of his work individually.

While students worked, I voiced over with tips:

- "Try saying, 'He probably thinks or feels . . .'"
- "Give evidence. What in the text makes you think that?"

LINK

Restate the teaching point. Rally students to use their limited reading time to choose a passage to reread, considering the author's point of view.

"Readers, this work of studying the author's point of view and how it's conveyed in the text is important whenever you are reading nonfiction. Understanding the author's point of view can help you to figure out why an author might have written a text, and it can also help you to think critically about the information that's included, to question why the author might have included one story and left out another one.

"Today, you'll only have about fifteen minutes to read. Instead of reading on about your topic, will you start by choosing a text to *reread* to determine the author's point of view? As you reread, be on the lookout for different ways your author is conveying her point of view. Use the cards to help you notice techniques the author uses, and invent new technique cards if you need them. After you reread an article, choose a new article on your topic to read. Off you go to get started!"

INDEPENDENT READING

Coach to lift the level of students' work. Support students who need more foundational work with author's point of view and students who are ready to talk and write academically about it.

As you send students off to reread articles and books to determine their authors' points of view, you might find students who need additional support with this skill. You might give those students a tip that helps limit the number of techniques they need to study. You might tell them, "One of the most powerful techniques you can use to determine an author's point of view is to study the author's word choice, particularly the words the author uses to talk about the topic. This can help you identify how the author think or feels." You might channel those students to reread a passage on the lookout for the words the author used to describe the topic, and then you could coach as they consider whether those words are more positive or negative. Then you could ask, "Based on these words, what might this author think and feel about this topic?"

Other students might be ready to be nudged into using more academic language to help them discuss the author's point of view in a text. You might prepare a small sheet of prompts to give to readers who are ready to talk and write more academically.

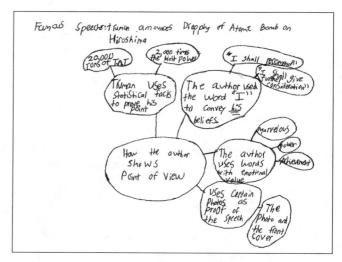

FIG. 18–1   Will analyzes a speech and notes the different techniques the author used to convey his point of view.

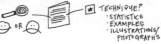

Analyzing the Impact of Authorial Techniques

"Researchers, we only have time for a very quick share today. Share the technique you noticed an author using that surprised you the most or that you thought had the biggest impact with someone sitting near you. Sometimes it's more hidden techniques that have the most power when we really stop to think about them. Off you go, turn and share."

SESSION 18 HOMEWORK

ATTENTING TO AUTHORS' POINTS OF VIEW AS YOU READ

Tonight, continue reading about your topic. Think about the central ideas the authors teach, the ideas you're growing, and all of the other ways you know to make the most of your nonfiction reading. In addition, will you pay particular attention to the techniques the authors use to get across a point of view? Do they choose to include certain quotes and leave others out? Do they tuck in small words that spark big emotions?

I'll send you home with a copy of the 'Techniques Authors Use to Convey a Point of View' chart so you can reference it as you read. Of course, you might discover other techniques authors use to communicate a point of view. Be sure to jot those down if you do so you can share them with your research group.

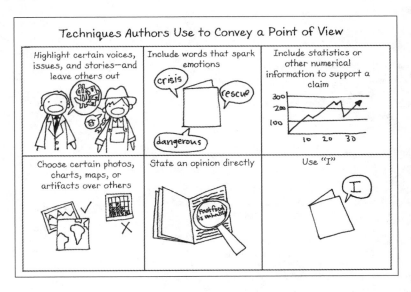

Dealing with Texts that Contradict Each Other

IN THIS SESSION

TODAY YOU'LL teach students that readers notice when texts directly contradict one another, and they study those texts closely to determine which is most trustworthy.

TODAY YOUR STUDENTS will regularly synthesize what they're learning across texts, and they'll draw on this work studying points of contradiction as needed.

MINILESSON

CONNECTION

Share a short text on your research topic that includes contradicting information. Ask students to consider how the information in this text contradicts what they've already learned.

"Last night, I was reading another text on GMOs. It's from a website called Kids Right to Know. I read the section called 'GMO Information,' and I came across some information that seemed to contradict what we read before. Listen for the information that contradicts what we already know."

What's a GMO?

A GMO (Genetically Modified Organism) is a laboratory process of taking genes from one species and inserting them into another in an attempt to obtain a desired trait or characteristic.

What kinds of genetically engineered traits have been added to our food crops?

- Herbicide tolerance crops, which lets the farmer spray weedkillers directly on the crop without killing it

- Pesticide-producing crops, where the plant produces its own internal pesticide

Why should you be concerned about GMOs?

- Various feeding studies in animals have resulted in tumors, damaged immune systems, smaller brains, livers, birth defects, reproductive problems and infertility

- GMOs have also been linked with allergies, various digestive and bowel syndromes and even autism in humans

"Tell your partner what information here contradicts what we've already read about GMOs." I gave students thirty seconds to talk, and then called them back together. "I heard you saying the other articles we've read about GMOs talk about how we don't know what GMOs health effects will be, but this article says GMOs cause all kinds of problems for humans. That feels like a big contradiction."

❖ **Name the teaching point.**

"Today I want to teach you that when readers notice texts that contradict one another in big or small ways, they can't just say, 'Hmm, that's interesting,' and then put those texts aside. Instead, they analyze the texts and decide which is more trustworthy."

TEACHING

Introduce a few tests a reader can give a text to judge its trustworthiness.

"To determine whether a text is trustworthy or not, it helps to give your text a few tests." I posted a list of tests and quickly talked through each one.

Demonstrate how you study a text to determine whether it can be trusted.

"So we've got two texts that contradict: 'The Battle Over GMOs' and 'GMO Information.' Will you help me take one of these texts, 'The Battle Over GMOs' and give it these tests? As we try these tests, be thinking about whether or not this text is trustworthy."

To Determine if a Text is Trustworthy...

☑ Check the <u>source</u>: Who published this text?

☑ Check the <u>author</u>: Who wrote this text? What's their background? Their experience with the topic?

☑ Check the <u>publication date</u>: When was this text written? Is it current?

☑ Check the <u>evidence</u>: Is evidence given to support the claim? Are sources cited?

☑ Check for <u>balance in the content</u>: Does it include multiple perspectives?

☑ Check the <u>author's purpose</u>: Why was this text likely written or recorded?

I displayed "The Battle Over GMOs." "Okay, so first we have to check the source. Who published this text? Well, I see at the top that this is from *The New York Times Upfront*. I know that's a magazine published by Scholastic and by the *New York Times*. Those are both organizations that do a ton of writing for adults and for kids."

I looked up at the chart. "Let's check the author: Alessandra Potenza. I don't know anything about her, do you? Let's search her name online." I searched her name, clicked on her website, pulled up the "About" page and said, "Oh, it says here she's a journalist who writes a lot about science stuff, and she's worked for a bunch of science places like *Science World* and *National Geographic*. Keep thinking about whether this text is trustworthy or not.

Keep your modeling here brief. Showing the process is far more important than learning about the journalist.

"Now we have to check the publication date. This was written on February 8, 2016. That's pretty current, especially considering GMOs have been around since 1994.

"Okay, now we have to look at the evidence, balance, and the author's likely purpose. I think as far as evidence, the author quotes a lot of experts and gives sources for research statistics, like the Pew Research Center. To me, the article seems balanced. Potenza included multiple perspectives. She quotes GMO experts who say GMOs are safe, and she quotes scientists who think GMOs will hurt the environment. And if I consider why this text was written, it seems like it was written to teach us about the different sides in the battle over GMOs. Her title and the questions she asks in her subtitle both fit with that."

Ask students to discuss whether or not the text is trustworthy.

"Well, what do you think? Is this text trustworthy? Think across all the tests we did to make your case to your partner." I gave students a minute to talk.

ACTIVE ENGAGEMENT

Rally students to study another text to determine whether it can be trusted.

"Let's compare that text to 'GMO Information.' I'll give you and your research group a copy of that text. Make sure at least one of you has a phone or another device in case you need to do a little research. Take a few minutes to give this text our 'To Determine if a Text is Trustworthy?' test, and come to an agreement about whether it can be trusted or not."

As students worked, I moved from group to group to coach:

Evaluating sources is challenging, lifelong work. Expect students to approximate this work here. Trust that they will have regular opportunities to practice this work moving forward.

- "Give the text each test before you make a decision about whether it's trustworthy or not."

- "If you can't find the author or a publication date, consider that when you're deciding whether to trust this text."

- "To figure out whether the text includes multiple perspectives, it helps to compare what one text teaches to other texts."

- "Consider why the author wrote this article. What was his or her purpose for writing?"

- "Think back to our work from yesterday. What are some techniques the author uses to promote her point of view? This might help you to understand the author's purpose and what she wants you to believe."

Many students commented on the author of the text, a school-aged food activist who seems to have an anti-GMO stance. Some commented that, although the current year is listed on the bottom of the website, it is difficult to tell when the article "GMO Information" was actually written. Some noticed that there is a list of links on the website, but they weren't sure whether the links support all of the article's claims. Some students wondered how to find out if it was really true that GMOs led to things like damaged immune systems and smaller brains. They noted there wasn't much evidence in the article to prove that claim.

Suggest partners compare the first text to the second text to determine which text is more trustworthy. Then, briefly recap their conclusions.

"Now that you've done a bit of research, will you and your partner determine which text is more trustworthy: 'GMO Information' or 'The Battle Over GMOs'? Be sure to explain why." I gave students about thirty seconds to talk. Students overwhelmingly agreed that "The Battle Over GMOs" was more trustworthy, because the source and the author could be trusted and because the content was more balanced.

"Readers, you've done some perceptive work here. You took a harder look at 'GMO Information,' and you noticed that the author has a clear stance against GMOs, so you surmised that the information here might not tell the whole story. You questioned the article's sources, and when it was written. As you'll remember from your research in the past, it's important to be extra cautious with websites. Anyone can publish a website, and many websites are biased and not well fact-checked. It could be that the information presented in the second article is true, but the author needs to present more proof of this before we can fully trust her claims."

LINK

Restate the teaching point, and send students off with a reminder to draw on a repertoire of work.

"Readers, whenever you notice that two texts contradict each other, study those two texts closely to determine which text is more trustworthy. Asking questions about the source, author, publication date, content, and language can help you to make this judgment well." I added the point to our anchor chart.

To Research a New Topic . . .

- Preview texts to identify repeating subtopics.
- Build up a bit of background knowledge quickly.
  - Sequence your texts. Start with easier texts–even videos!
  - Teach others what you're learning.
- Create a brief summary of the text.
  - Ask, "What's the author's central idea?"
  - Determine main ideas that support the central idea.
  - Say back the central and main ideas in a short paragraph.
- Synthesize across texts.
  - Fit with?
  - Extends?
  - Contradicts?
- Turn to outside resources to clear up confusions.
- Become an expert on the topic's lingo.
- Grow your own ideas about what you're reading.
- **Study parts where texts contradict. Determine which text is most trustworthy.**

When texts contradict, determine which is most trustworthy.

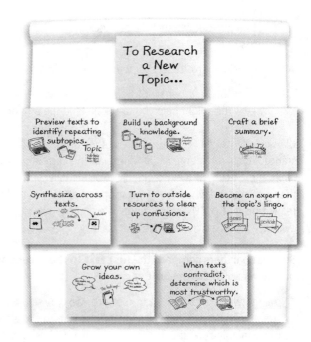

"Now, you'll only need to do this work when you find texts that contradict one another. Otherwise, you'll want to keep reading, drawing on the other work you know readers do whenever they research a topic. Off you go!"

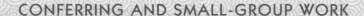

Flexibly Drawing on the Work of the Unit and Reading Critically

TODAY, ON THIS SECOND-TO-LAST SESSION IN THE UNIT, take a moment to take stock of all the work your students (and you!) have done. Hopefully the work they learned in this unit's previous bends is becoming automatic. Hopefully they are flexibly orienting themselves to their texts, determining and rethinking central ideas, building background knowledge as they research, summarizing, synthesizing across texts, and developing more independence in their reading and research process.

As this unit draws to a close, students have moved into the terrain of critical literacy: beginning to question the sources of texts and develop their own ideas as they read. Continue to support them as they read and research today, both in flexibly applying the foundational skills of the unit and in taking steps toward critically evaluating their texts. Your goal is to support the kind of thinking that will lead your students to pause when confronted with the next viral Tweet or video and consider, "Is this real? Is there evidence to support it? What might the author of this want me to think?"

Separating Fact from Opinion

In the more complex texts that middle school students are expected to read, it can be difficult to separate fact from opinion. In most of the texts they encounter, the author's opinion will be inserted as subtle, implied statements. To determine which parts of an article are fact and which are opinion, a reader must often make inferences, looking for clues that signal an author's stance. As you confer, you might keep on the lookout for readers who could benefit from a refresher on fact versus opinion. Brainstorm a quick list together of the qualities of a fact (is measurable, observable, is known to exist, etc.) and the qualities of an opinion (is an assumption, is a point of view, etc.). Then walk them through a short section from an article, analyzing each sentence to determine whether it is a fact or an opinion. You might have students use different-colored highlighters for facts and opinions, so that they can analyze the section at a glance to determine whether it is mostly fact or mostly opinion. This might help them to understand the purpose of the article as a whole.

Sequencing Texts from Completely Trustworthy to Completely Untrustworthy

If you notice a club of students investigating whether their texts are trustworthy or not, you might introduce them to a tool that helps them compare the trustworthiness of their sources by sequencing them. After investigating their sources individually, students could lay them out on a progression made out of a sentence strip, with *completely trustworthy* on one end and *completely untrustworthy* on the other end. You might show them how you examine a text to determine where it might fit on the progression. Encourage students to compare the trustworthiness of texts, and to make a case for why they are placing each text at a particular point on the progression. You might give them sentence starters to support this work.

> *This text is more trustworthy than . . . because . . .*
>
> *This text is less trustworthy than . . . because . . .*

Leave clubs with the sentence strip progression, and encourage them to keep sequencing the new texts they investigate.

Analyzing Why Authors Choose Different Content to Emphasize

Some students might note points of contradiction, and might evaluate their texts for their trustworthiness, but might need support in coming to conclusions about the authors' purposes. In this case, you might gather these students to extend their work. You could say, "Today I want to teach you that when you're thinking across texts, you can pay attention to what the authors decide to emphasize and write a lot about and what they exclude or barely mention. After you notice these parts, you can consider why the author might have emphasized or excluded that information."

Then, you could briefly explain how you did this work. You might say, "The other day, I was studying the 'Seeing Red: The Flavr Savr Tomato' video and 'The Battle Over GMOs.' I realized that 'The Battle Over GMOs' talked *way more* about the problems people have with GMOs than the 'Seeing Red' video did. I had to think about why the author might have done that. It could be that the author of 'Seeing Red' doesn't really think that there are many problems with GMOs."

You'll want to quickly channel students to try this work. You might say, "Right now, will you choose an article you're familiar with and study it? What information did the author really emphasize, and write a lot about? Is there information that the author left out? Once you've noticed what the author included and excluded, consider why the author might have done that." You could give students a few minutes to work on their own, and then channel them to talk with a partner.

As you coach in, you might say:

- "Reread the article first to see what the author *included* and said the most about."
- "Reread to see what the author excluded. What have you read about in other articles that this author left out?"
- "It might help to compare your article to another article. What did that author choose to include versus this author?"
- "Consider a few reasons why the author might have done that. Try saying, 'Maybe . . . Could it be . . . Perhaps . . .'?"

Helping Students to Compare and Contrast across Texts

As students become more adept at considering how the content of two texts fits together or contradicts, you might gather students together to lift the level of their compare-and-contrast work by showing them a mini-chart listing a range of ways readers can compare and contrast.

If students would benefit from a demonstration, you could choose a particular focus, and show students how you compare and contrast two familiar texts with this focus in mind. If students need extra scaffolding, you might ask them to first try the work together, using the shared texts from the minilesson, before they try it in their own books. With a partner, they could choose a way to compare the two texts—content, structure, craft, perspective—and then talk about how the two texts are similar and different related to that focus.

Letting Contradictions Spark Further Research

After evaluating the trustworthiness of texts that contradict, you might notice some students naturally letting inconsistencies between texts guide them to conduct further research. Encourage these students to formulate new research questions and to add their learning to their notes. You might also encourage them to write about their findings to determine their own ideas about the contradictions they are researching.

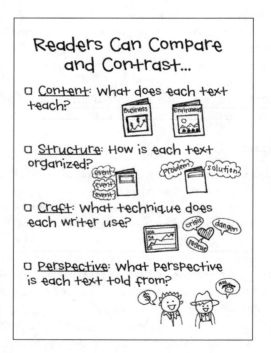

Supporting Student-Run Research Groups

Encourage research groups to make their own decisions about how to best use their time.

"Readers, instead of giving you direction about what you and your research club should do today, you'll be in charge. It will be up to you to talk and make a decision about what your club needs.

"Let me remind you of some options. You might decide to use your time to talk. If you decide to talk, look over our charts to get ideas about what you might discuss. We've talked a lot lately about author's perspective, so maybe you have some burning thoughts about this that you'd like to share. Or, maybe you've just read a new article and are dying to share some of the information you learned. It could also be that you would like more time to read. Maybe you're all in the middle of articles or books, and you want to read on today so you have more to talk about tomorrow. Finally, you may want to use this time to write long to grow some of the ideas you're having after evaluating the trustworthiness of texts today. You may decide to record some of your own perspectives about your topic.

"Make a decision with your group about how you will spend your time, and then get started!"

Source: National Geographic kids.
National geo kids is a trustworthy site because it made other articles that I have used.

author: A group basically wrote this text, that means that there were a whole lot of information that was put together to create this article.

Publication date: This text was written in March 17th 2015. This text is ~~pretty~~ current because it was written about 2 years ago.

Evidence: All the sources were used to support the claim, the evidence introduced difficulties, that was used to back up, "would you have survived the titanic?" Also, some of the sources were sited.

Balance in the content: This article included many prospectives from Captain Edward John smith and his crew, to Milvina Dean who has been through the titanics and has shared her story.

Author's purpose: This text is written to give examples and to back up "would you have survived the titanic?" It doesn't introduce, this is written for money, but for information purposes.

I rate this article a ~~9/10~~ for trustworthyness.

FIG. 19–1   David tests a text to determine whether it is trustworthy and decides it can be rated 9/10 for trustworthiness.

PREPARING FOR TED-STYLE TALKS

You're such experts on your topics that tomorrow, I want to make sure you have an opportunity to teach others about what you're learning. You'll be giving a four- or five-minute TED-style talk, which is a talk focused on a topic, where you teach critical information related to your topic using visuals and gestures and more. Usually, these talks are interesting and engaging for the listeners.

Tonight, will you spend some time getting ready for that talk so you're prepared to plan and deliver it tomorrow? Think about what work will most pay off for you, and then do those things as you read tonight. You might consider:

- Are there articles or books on your topic that you still need to read?

- Are there articles that were too tricky to read a few days ago that you want to reread now that you have some background knowledge on your topic?

- Do you have research questions you haven't answered yet, so you need to spend some time researching further?

- Are there big ideas you're growing for which you need to find more supports?

Crafting TED Talks to Get Others Fascinated by Your Topic

ear Teachers,

Over the last week, your students investigated a second topic, synthesizing information across texts to learn as much as they could, this time with greater independence. There is an enormous amount to celebrate as you bring this unit to a close, and so this celebration, your final one, merits something special. Above all, you'll want students to feel ownership of their knowledge and to have the confidence to teach it to others.

Teaching others has multiple benefits. In a *Time* magazine article titled "The Protégé Effect," Annie Murphy Paul examined how people have known for centuries that teaching others helps to solidify their own knowledge. The Roman philosopher Seneca said, "When you teach others, you learn." In addition, if students teach others about their topics, their talks will serve as informal sales pitches, enticing other students to want to learn more about those topics.

If you decide to set students up to share their knowledge about the topics they've been researching through TED-style talks, you'll want to keep them simple. We recommend they be quick, informal talks, and that you have students plan and deliver their talks in the course of a single reading workshop.

To build excitement about giving TED-style talks, you might show students one of the many TED talks appropriate for middle-schoolers as a model. A quick Internet search of "best TED talks for middle-schoolers" will yield lots of great examples from which to choose, such as "The Danger of a Single Story" by Chimamanda Ngozi Adichie, Ben Kacyra's talk on ancient wonders captured in 3-D, or Christien Meindertsma's talk on how pig parts make the world turn. Students could watch the TED talk with an inquiry question in mind. "What does this TED talk speaker do that we could also do?" Encourage them to move beyond simply taking in the content of the talk to observing how the speaker teaches the information.

After students watch, you might chart some of what they noticed the speaker doing, such as:

- Highlighting central ideas clearly and early on
- Separating the talk into subtopics and talking long about each subtopic
- Using visuals
- Including a variety of rich details, such as dates, statistics, quotes, and study results
- Adding anecdotes and/or humor
- Leaving the audience with a summary and perhaps a call to action

You could also references passages from *Talk Like TED: The 9 Public-Speaking Secrets of the World's Top Minds* by Carmine Gallo. If you want to build excitement, you might share Gallo's opinion that "ideas are the currency of the twenty-first century. Your ideas will change the direction of your life and potentially change the world" (pp. 247–48). If you want to help students lift the level of their speeches, you could share the three components to an engaging presentation. Gallo says, "The most engaging presentations are: Emotional— They touch my heart.; Novel—they teach me something new.; Memorable—They present content in ways I'll never forget" (p. 8).

This session will work best if you give students about the first half of the period to prepare for their talks individually and then leave the second half of the period for them to give their talks. To prepare, students might first reread their notes, then create an outline of what they'll teach and in what order, and then mark up images and charts they want to include in their talk. Encourage them to plan for about four to five minutes of speaking.

Once students have planned their TED talks, channel them into informal groups to teach and learn from one another. You might form groups with four to five students who each researched a different topic. Rally students to listen to the TED talks given by their classmates, thinking, "What big things am I learning that will stay with me?" and "Which topics sound fascinating, like ones I'd like to read and learn more about?" Yes, this unit is coming to a close, but your goal is to build lifelong avid nonfiction readers, and you'll want to encourage your students to pursue new topics of inquiry, not just in future nonfiction units, but on their own time.

While students teach, you might move from group to group, listening with rapt engagement, displaying your fascination with students' topics and teaching. You might scrawl some favorite quotes as students teach, so that you can share them out later. To wrap up, give students a few minutes to jot and reflect on what they learned. They might note questions they have about a topic or two that they could pose to their classmates later, or research on their own down the line. If there's time, kids might even share out some of their reflections, not just about one another's topics, but about the unit as a whole.

MA	Ted Talk- Melati & Isabel Wijsen-Mentor	
	Structure	Style
	• Starts by talking about how they started thinking about the issue their supporting	• They use hand motions
		• Have eye contact with the audience
	• They ask retorical questions	• Uses visuals to help support their thinking
	• Explains how they became part of this foundation	• Uses humor
	• Taught the audience a lesson	• Used pauses, and they didn't talk over each other/ they talked the same amount (one voice didn't overpower the other)
	• They prompted a problem and then gave a solution	

FIG. 20–1 Paige jots notes about the structure and style of a TED talk.

Of course, you'll also want to set aside a little time to celebrate and reflect on the unit with your colleagues. You might gather students' reading notebooks, and spend some time studying their jots, looking for footprints of your teaching. Do you see evidence that students are revising their thinking about a text or topic as they read on? Do you see evidence that students are synthesizing information across texts on a topic? Do you see evidence that students are considering point of view as they read? Think about the major focuses of your teaching, and look for evidence of those areas in students' work.

To teaching and learning!
Katie

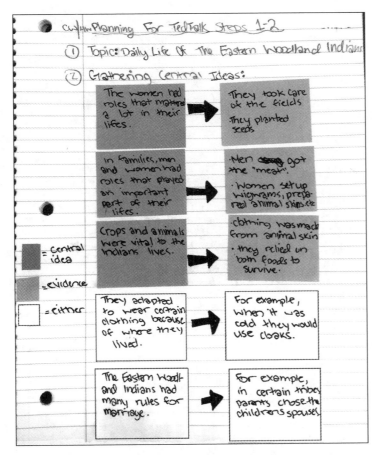

FIG. 20–2 As part of her social studies class, Molly prepares for a TED-style talk on the Eastern Woodland Indians by recording central ideas and key evidence.